PENGUIN BOOKS

MARRIAGE INSIDE OUT

Christopher Clulow and Janet Mattinson are both psychoanalytic marital therapists who have practised, taught and undertaken research at the Tavistock Marital Studies Institute. They each began their professional life in social work; Christopher Clulow was in the probation service and Janet Mattinson worked in child care before becoming a lecturer in social work at the University of Exeter. In 1987 Christopher Clulow succeeded Janet Mattinson as Chairman of the Tavistock Marital Studies Institute.

In their time at the Institute they have written extensively on the subject of marriage and marital therapy. Christopher Clulow is the author of *To Have and To Hold: Marriage, the First Baby and Preparing Couples for Parenthood* (1982), *Marital Therapy: An Inside View* (1985) and, with Christopher Vincent, *In the Child's Best Interests: Divorce Court Welfare and the Search for a Settlement* (1987). He is also the editor of *Marriage: Disillusion and Hope* (1990) and *Rethinking Marriage* (1993). Janet Mattinson's publications include *Marriage and Mental Handicap* (1970), *The Reflection Process in Casework Supervision* (1977), *Work, Love and Marriage* (1988) and, with Ian Sinclair, *Mate and Stalemate: Working with Marital Problems in a Social Services Department* (1979).

Christopher Clulow is Chairman of the Commission on Marriage and Interpersonal Relations of the International Union of Family Organizations and a member of the editorial advisory boards of *Family and Conciliation Courts Review*, the *Journal of Social Work Practice* and *Sexual and Marital Therapy*. He lives in St Albans with his wife and two children.

Janet Mattinson is a Jungian analyst, and is now retired and lives in Cumbria.

Marriage Inside Out

CHRISTOPHER CLULOW
and
JANET MATTINSON

Revised Edition

PENGUIN BOOKS

PENGUIN BOOKS

Published by the Penguin Group
Penguin Books Ltd, 27 Wrights Lane, London W8 5TZ, England
Penguin Books USA Inc., 375 Hudson Street, New York, New York 10014, USA
Penguin Books Australia Ltd, Ringwood, Victoria, Australia
Penguin Books Canada Ltd, 10 Alcorn Avenue, Toronto, Ontario, Canada M4V 3B2
Penguin Books (NZ) Ltd, 182–190 Wairau Road, Auckland 10, New Zealand

Penguin Books Ltd, Registered Offices: Harmondsworth, Middlesex, England

First published 1989
Revised edition 1995
10 9 8 7 6 5 4 3 2 1

Printed in England by Clays Ltd, St Ives plc
Filmset in Linotron Bembo 9/11pt

Contents

Acknowledgements

The ideas contained in this book come from many different sources, and for the most part we lay no claim to originality of thought. As always, the couples who have come to us for help have been our best teachers. We have drawn on the experience of some of them, although we have ensured that they cannot be identified. Our approach bears the hallmark of the Tavistock Institute of Marital Studies, and we owe debts of gratitude to our colleagues past and present. In particular we would like to thank Patricia Coussell, Lynne Cudmore, Barbara Dearnley and Diana Daniell for permission to draw on papers they prepared for a conference organized by the Institute under the title 'A Natural History of Marriage' (held, appropriately enough, at London Zoo). Diana Daniell has also agreed to our quoting her thesis on transitions in marriage.

The book was written during a period of transition for us: one of us relinquished the Chair of the Institute on retirement; the other took it on. With our separate preoccupations we worked more independently of each other than might otherwise have been the case, and we are indebted to Elma Sinclair for helping us to 'marry up' our different manuscripts, in terms both of content and style. We owe much to Benita Dyal and Margaret Spooner for their professionalism and sheer hard work in assembling the manuscript against the clock, and during a period when there were so many other pressing responsibilities to attend to. And we take this opportunity to thank Margaret Spooner for serving us both so efficiently and faithfully in her double role of administrator and chairman's secretary.

Finally, we wish to thank the Family Policy Studies Centre for their help in making available information concerning trends in family life for Britain and other countries. The excerpt from 'I Do, I Will, I Have', by Ogden Nash, is reprinted from 'I Wouldn't Have Missed It' and *Versus*, 1949, by permission of André Deutsch Ltd and Curtis Brown Ltd.

Christopher Clulow   Janet Mattinson

London   Temple Sowerby

September 1988

1.   The Marriage Maze

'Marriage is a great institution,' quipped Mae West, 'but I'm not ready for an institution yet.' Most of us are, however, if the figures are to be believed. In Britain the great majority of people marry at some point in their lives. There were 350,000 marriages in 1991, and the number of marriages contracted each year has been remarkably constant over the past quarter of a century. Yet there are signs that marriage is losing its popularity. High levels of divorce, falling marriage rates, increasing cohabitation and the rapid growth in one-parent households suggest that all is not well with the institution. Yet while men and women marry later than they did twenty years ago, and while marriage is likely to be preceded by a period of living together, the institution of marriage is statistically more common today than it was in Victorian times, that period of our history which is so frequently presented as the golden age of the family.

The recent trends in family life are remarkably similar in other Western societies. In the United States, Canada, Australia, New Zealand and western Europe there has been a fall in marriage and remarriage rates, an increase in cohabitation and a tendency for marriage and parenthood to be postponed; family size has become smaller and married women with children have participated more in the labour force. Despite these changes marriage has not gone out of fashion.

Yet marriages frequently fail. There were just over 171,000 divorces in the United Kingdom in 1991. Along with Denmark, Britain has the highest divorce rate in the European community, and predictions indicate that two in five marriages contracted today will founder, over half of these in the first nine years. Similar predictions have been made for other western countries, and in the USA and the Soviet Union the odds on marriages breaking down are said to be as high as one in two. Although the number of marriages overall has remained steady in Britain, in 1991 only 63 per cent were first-time marriages as compared with 79 per cent in 1971. Among the married, the single and the divorced there is a hunger for advice about how to sustain intimate relationships, and the queue at the doctor's surgery and outside the counsellor's door is growing ever longer. Is marriage a secure institution, or is it on the decline? If it has become a problematic enterprise why should this be – or are we now seeing what has always been there but has previously been obscured from view? What is it that keeps drawing people into making such a risky commitment? Are we hidebound by social convention or fascinated by our misfortunes?

For most or us, statistics about marriage and divorce are of no great concern. What does concern us is our own marriage, particularly when we are about to embark on it or when we enter a period of difficulty. Then we are likely to ask whether our experiences are part of the ordinary trials and tribulations of married life, or whether we have a Marital Problem. The distinction is seldom clear cut. Many of the 100,000 or so couples who approach English marriage guidance councils for help each year are seeking reassurance that their problems are not unique and might actually be 'normal'. Most will be disappointed in this respect, not because their problems are particularly unusual but because the social changes of the past thirty years have made it extremely difficult for anyone to speak with authority about what constitutes 'normal' married life. This uncertainty generates its own problems. It has led to conflict between the wish to order our lives in the way we choose and a craving for guidelines laid down by others.

So it is likely to be with some ambivalence that readers will pick up this book. There will be both a wish for and a resistance to any prescriptions for managing the problems of marriage. Prescriptions there will be none, although we hope that this book will help to answer some of the questions which puzzle and disturb those who wrestle with the inherently problematic business of being married. Through exploring the private domain of marriage, and the personal motives and meanings individuals bring to it, we can offer some explanations for why the ordinary problems of married life escalate into Marital Problems in some cases and not in others. The struggles which engage happily married couples and those whose unhappy experience may cause them to part are essentially the same. Only the solutions are different.

In this book we shall be exploring the informal ties of marriage, the personal and psychological roots of a relationship which can so critically sustain, or fail to sustain, the individuals legally bound together. In writing primarily about psychological aspects of marriage relationships, we are concerned with unconscious as well as conscious processes of the mind which influence people's behaviour. We do not distinguish the two processes as totally different orders of thought and feeling. People vary in their capacity for introspection. Some people are more conscious than others of their underlying hopes, motives, fears and fantasies. What is conscious for one person can be unconscious for another. For some readers this book may formulate what they already know. For others it may put into words what they know in their bones.

Some theorists believe that what can be labelled as 'disturbed behaviour', 'mental illness' or 'madness' is of a different order from 'normal' behaviour and mental health. From our theoretical stance, we understand behaviour, average or extreme, to be on a continuum, with the 'normal' representing a middle point with extremes on either side. What distinguishes the middle from the extremes is, first, the ability to feel the full range of feelings within the human capacity, even when they conflict with one another; and second, the ability to handle these feelings (albeit with difficulty at times) in a relatively flexible manner and without being destructive either to oneself or to others. It is an absence of certain feelings, or an excessive strength of feeling and the subsequent inflexibility of response, which distinguishes most forms of mental ill-health. So it is not that 'normal' people never feel greedy, envious, jealous or even murderous, but that they are not compelled to wear their feelings on their sleeves nor express them in actions. At one end of the continuum, people who dare not recognize their own feelings may be in as much difficulty as those at the other end whose feelings are out of control.

It may seem to the reader that much of this book is only about *problems* and pays less attention to the fact that many couples remain not only satisfied with their marriage, but enormously enriched by it. We believe that the interactive processes described in this book are common to all people, but are more subtle, and therefore less noticeable, when they occur in loving and satisfying marriages than when a relationship runs into trouble. As one headmaster said in the days of 'approved' (reform) schools, 'If you want to understand what goes on at Eton, better to come and first observe my establishment for delinquents. It's all the same, just more blown up.' Along with those who are worried about their problems, readers who are well-satisfied and sustained by their marriages may find interest in what may be for them a new way of looking at the subject.

We shall concentrate on first marriages, recognizing that subsequent marriages have special problems which we have not room to address here – although much of what we say is still relevant. Similarly we have not attempted to explore marriage as it exists in non-western cultures and amongst ethnic groups in our own country. It is enough to try to understand the differences in one broad culture. Although the few historical and statistical facts we have detailed are British ones, most are comparable with those for other western countries. However, comparing figures from different countries can be a dangerous game, as they are often compiled from different bases and in different ways. The figures which we refer to are therefore the ones with which we are most familiar, namely those pertaining to Britain. At the present time, Britain and other western societies are in a turbulent phase. When the 'baby' of a marriage is in trouble, it can get lost in the turbulence of the 'bathwater' of an environment which is in flux.

BABIES AND BATHWATER

Imagine, then, a not uncommon occurrence. The time is six-thirty in the evening, a notoriously low point in the day for couples with young children. A mother is bathing her young daughter. It has been a long day. This fact is reflected in the tired replies the little girl gets to her self-preoccupied chatter as she builds mountains out of the foamy soapsuds created by her bubble bath. The stillness of the little girl's self-absorption and the mother's tiredness is broken by the sound of the front door shutting, signalling father's return home from work. The day has not gone well for him. He feels an unreasonable sense of irritation building up in him when no one is downstairs to greet him and there is no sign of supper. He joins his wife and daughter in the bathroom and is further irritated by the languid atmosphere which contrasts with the frenetic activity of his day. Against his better instincts he makes a critical remark which leads to an altercation between him and his wife. The tension in the bathroom increases and the little girl splashes water over the side of the bath. Annoyed at getting wet, and anxious to hurry things along, her father yanks the plug out of the bath, allowing the water to begin draining away. The little girl leaps to her feet and bursts into hysterical crying. Clinging to her mother, she begs to be rescued from the plug-hole man who will gobble her up if she stays in the bath. The row between the parents escalates as the little girl's mother begins to dry her down. She accuses her husband of upsetting the child. He retaliates fiercely, believing his wife is trying to turn his daughter against him by making him into some kind of ogre. The tensions of the day have now found a focus in the marriage and from here on anything is possible.

Ordinarily, we recognize these conflicts for what they are. She looks forward to the prospect of some relief from the demanding business of caring for children which his return from work seems to promise. He is weighed down by his commitments outside the home and looks forward to a meal awaiting him on the table. Each looks to the other for respite, and each reacts with a sense of hurt and rejection when it is not forthcoming. There is no welcome hug for her, no welcoming meal for him. The hoped-for support and understanding response dissolve into the gurglings of the plug-hole man. The turbulence may settle quickly, or the agitation may last for hours before calm is restored. Sometimes the incident will touch on underlying sensitivities, feeding suspicions and providing confirmation of what had always been feared: 'He's only concerned about himself.' 'She can't be depended on for anything.' 'He isn't really interested in me.' 'She doesn't want to know.'

When this happens, the ordinary tensions of life are inflated into major conflicts. The more frequently they occur, the more ingrained becomes the notion that something is wrong with the marriage. What happens then is hard to predict. Some people choose to disengage a little, continuing their daily routines and ignoring their own feelings or any signals from their partner. Some interpret their difficulties as evidence that they have made a mistake and then proceed to jettison the marriage. Some thrash out their differences together, maybe with the help of an outsider, and succeed in bringing about sufficient change to sustain hope for a better future.

As marital therapists, we have heard many couples recount episodes similar to the one we have described. Attempting to justify their behaviour to themselves, to each other and to us, they search for an explanation of why they feel so strongly about relatively trivial occurrences. True, a more serious infidelity may provide the catalyst for opening up previously closed channels of communication, although more frequently it will close them down. Yet we have been impressed by how much can be learned from discussing the mundane and the ordinary. As couples talk about their problems, we hear the assumptions we all can make about why people behave as they do in marriage. As we listen, we hear how very differently others can perceive and interpret the same behaviour. The scope for making discoveries about ourselves and others through discussing the different feelings, attitudes and reactions prompted by the ordinary machinations of everyday married life is one reason for writing this book. But we recognize how difficult it can be to talk about these things, and the courage it sometimes takes.

One result of our experience has been to make us extremely cautious in making judgements about what is a good and what is a bad marriage. Situations that we might regard as intolerable do not always create the problems for others that we would anticipate. Similarly, what we might see as a good living arrangement would not necessarily carry much appeal for others. To use the bathwater analogy, some people prefer to make waves, others prefer to soak silently; and there is a considerable variety of view about what constitutes a comfortable temperature. What seems to us to be important is that the conscious and unconscious arrangements couples make in their lives together should not be at the expense of either partner's integrity. Paradoxically, marital conflict is not only a threat to integrity, but is necessary for the development of an integrated self. How can we learn about ourselves and others except by relating to people who are close to us yet different from us? Sometimes a faultily constructed view of ourselves has to fall apart before it can be correctly reassembled. The frictions of domestic living can provide a spur for learning. In this sense marital conflict has a creative side, and it becomes important not to throw out the baby of a developing marriage with the bathwater of its growing pains.

INSIDES AND OUTSIDES

Marriage is a social and a psychological institution. It is a bridge between public and private worlds. To understand adequately what is happening outside marriage involves taking account of the private relationships between men and women. Equally, the private face of marriage has to be understood in the context of the social environment in which couples live out their lives together.

The social landscape has changed considerably in the course of this century, and particularly in the past thirty years. Today, in the west, a much higher proportion of women marry than did a hundred or so years ago. In mid-Victorian England almost a third of women between twenty-two and forty were spinsters, mostly because of a shortage of men. Spinster was almost a term of abuse. Now, low infant-mortality rates, as well as forty years without a major war, have radically changed the balance between the sexes, so that by the year 2000 there will be a large and growing pool of bachelors and a shortage of spinsters. Moreover, women today have more options than marriage when considering what to do with their lives. For the first time there are signs that men are more anxious to marry than women. Will 'bachelor' become a term of abuse in the future?

Changing patterns of sexual behaviour mean that it is now no longer necessary to marry before admitting to a sexual relationship. More couples are living together outside the formal framework of marriage than did even fifteen years ago, although the indications are that cohabitation is more likely to be a prelude than an alternative to marriage. Of first-time marriages taking place today, more than half of the women will already have lived with their spouses (as compared with 8 per cent in the early 1970s). Many more couples live together in the period between one marriage ending and another beginning. Overall, 18 per cent of unmarried women and men between the ages of eighteen and sixty were in a cohabiting partnership in 1992. In other countries private legal contracts are drawn up by some couples in place of marriage. In this country, whether following a period of cohabitation or not, there is still a marked preference for making a public statement about the commitment by *getting married*.

The frequency with which people still choose to underpin their personal promises with public vows emphasizes the social significance with which marriage is imbued. It makes no sense to separate the personal from the social when thinking about marriage because each dimension affects the other. Marriage, in essence, contains and expresses the personal and the collective. In microcosm, men and women fashion out a social world as they make their lives together and, perhaps later, start to build a family of their own. Marriage provides a bridge between his inner world and hers, his understanding of himself and her understanding of herself. In the process of bridging the gap between two individuals, a new collective identity is forged. Not only does marriage contain the individual identities of 'he' and 'she', but it is also a statement of a third and joint identity: 'they' as a couple, and, later, 'they' as a family. Sometimes the collective identity is fostered and its claims promoted over and above those of the individual. Concern to present a united front may stifle the expression of personal differences. Conversely, individuality may be so rigorously safeguarded that outsiders may express surprise upon learning of there being a marriage at all.

Tensions arising out of differing expectations, attitudes and perceptions (about who does the housework, how Sundays should be spent, how frequently relatives need visiting) are played out not only against the changing backcloth of the couple's partnership, but also in the wider context of social relationships. These include parents, grandparents, brothers, sisters, friends, workmates, churchmen, social workers, doctors, policemen, tax inspectors, social-security officials, lawyers and politicians, to name just a few. Magazines, newspapers, radio, film and television also play an important part in defining the culture in which couples make their marriages. Sometimes these external influences will support couples as they set about selecting from the seemingly endless range of choices which follow from the decision to marry. Sometimes they will complicate matters. Regardless of how their effects are felt, by acting as a bridge between couples and the society to which they belong, marriage becomes public as well as private property.

At no time is this more true than when marriages start and end. Most couples marrying for the first time wish to make an event of their wedding. The event is usually social rather than religious. Just over half of those living in England and Wales choose to get married in church, but it has been estimated that only one in seven of the grooms and one in four of the brides do so for strictly religious reasons. More likely, they view the marriage service as a symbolic affirmation and public acknowledgement of the importance of the occasion. Marriage is one of life's major events. The families and friends of both bride and groom usually want to convene to witness, support and celebrate this major step. They also want to mark the changes in roles and family relationships brought about by the wedding. Sons and daughters become husbands and wives; they also acquire in-laws and new positions in the families they have joined.

Throughout history, marriage has been recognized by the presence of at least one public witness to the vows made between a man and a woman.[1] The identity and allegiance of that witness has varied over time. In this country, until the Hardwicke Marriage Act of 1753, the Church of England competed with a variety of folk rituals which, done correctly, legitimized marriage. When property and financial interests were at stake, parents and family were likely to take an active interest in selecting the bride and groom. Yet in the sixteenth and seventeenth century, betrothal was often more significant than marriage itself. Parents were frequently absent from the ceremony, the couple's friends being the only audience to witness the betrothal vows.

Betrothal ceremonies served the social function of separating from the pool of eligible young men and women couples who had made a commitment to each other, and gave them permission to live in intimate seclusion. The wedding, when it came, was the political event which welcomed them back to social life and to their economic rights and responsibilities. As late as the nineteenth century the rite of the 'besom' wedding (which involved jumping a broomstick in public) was, in some quarters, sufficient entitlement to the rights of marriage. These 'broomstick couplings' disappeared when the 1836 Marriage Act came into force and introduced, for the first time, civil marriage witnessed by a registrar. It also marked the beginning of a central register of births, deaths and marriages. Today, couples marrying in a registry office or nonconformist church do so under the present-day successor to that Act, the 1949 Marriage Act. The wording of their promises is spelt out in section 44, although in language a little less eloquent than that coined by Archbishop Thomas Cranmer in the Book of Common Prayer, which, with one or two minor changes, is still used in Church of England weddings.

As well as attracting public attention at its inception, marriage becomes a matter of public concern when it breaks down. Along with the private distress there is public reaction. Although horns are no longer presented to cuckolded husbands, or smelly bushes festooned around the doors and windows of unchaste wives, people still feel upset and uneasy when those they know decide to part. A broken marriage imposes change on their lives too. While friends and relatives may be sympathetic, they often do not welcome the confusion and social disruption which can follow. This may be especially true if their own marriages are fragile; the break-up of another marriage can reactivate problems of their own. It is not unusual for marital breakdown to have a domino effect among groups of couples who have been used to spending much time in each other's company.

Despite social concern about marriage breakdown, there is a degree of ambivalence about the kind and source of help which should be made available to troubled marriages. Families and friends can often be helpful, although the fact that they have vested interests in the fortunes of those close to them (and prejudices about them) may limit their usefulness. It takes courage to seek out counselling help, and there may be suspicion about the methods and motives of professional helpers. Certainly there is some paranoia about the state becoming active in relation to affairs of the heart. In 1979 the British popular press responded to a government report on the marriage guidance services[2] by panning the prospect of a 'Minister for Marriage', a proposal which was not actually contained in the report.

Public disquiet is at its strongest when marriage breakdown involves children. There is concern about how they will weather the consequences of divorce, their immediate distress, and also the possible long-term effects upon them and the implications for future generations. This concern is built into the law of the land. Divorce judges have to satisfy themselves that arrangements made for children following the separation of their parents are the best possible in the circumstances. Only then can they make a divorce final. In England and Wales seven out of ten divorcing couples have children, and in around 10 per cent of these cases concern will be sufficient for judges to order a welfare report on the family before making a decision. This is a considerable intrusion upon the privacy of family life, and one justified solely by the need to safeguard the welfare of children.[3]

For other reasons there will be social concern about divorce. Building society managers do not relish the increased likelihood of having to re-possess mortgaged property because of the financial disasters which so often follow the breakdown of marriage. Church leaders show concern about high divorce rates, linking them with evidence of moral and spiritual decline in the country. Politicians decry the additional claims on the public purse when one economically viable home splits into two financially dependent households. In excess of £100m are spent annually in Britain on legal aid for resolving family issues in court. More than four times that sum is spent on supplementary benefit each year, the principal means of support for many one-parent households today. Once the indirect costs of maintaining medical, psychiatric and social services are taken into account, and if days lost at work and expenditure on drugs are used as yardsticks, the financial cost of marital problems becomes unquantifiable. The repercussions of marriage breakdown upon social institutions have led some to regard the phenomenom of divorce as a threat to the security of the state itself. Traditionally, the family has been regarded as the basic building block of a stable and responsible society, and until recently there has been little dissent from the view that marriage is the cornerstone of family life.

Marriage, then, contains a variety of personal and social meanings. Because it occupies a particularly sensitive position on the boundary between public and private aspects of life it is subject to many stresses. Couples bring to marriage the models of partnership they have learned from their parents and a legacy of experience about how to behave in, and what to expect from, intimate relationships. Two differently formed expectations are brought into a marriage. In their relationship with each other, partners will mediate and manage these differences to better or worse effect. Because marriage also provides a different sort of bridge between couples and their wider social and economic world, the social functions it performs will be peculiarly susceptible to environmental and cultural change. There can be little doubt that the accelerating pace of technological development, which has burst upon this century with the impact of what has been termed 'future shock', has had an effect upon marriage. A culture which accepts transience, demands novelty, and believes that life is best lived in the fast lane, cannot but affect our expectations of relationships. Secure gender and sexual identities are dependent upon having a recognized place and making a satisfying contribution in the community. As the community changes in response to social and economic forces, so does what it means to be a man or a woman. Marriage plays a part in facilitating and resisting these changes.

In the light of these pressures it may seem quite remarkable that two out of every three marriages contracted in the west today can expect to survive until the death of one of the partners, that in many of these marriages men and women will be emotionally engaged and satisfied with each other, and that their relationship will be sustained by more than habit. Statistically, it may well be that the stability of marriage is little different from what it was at other times in our history. The facts that we live longer, draw from a larger pool of potential partners and have more economic independence than most of our forebears increase our range of choices. These choices are structured less by social communication than in the past. Add to this the inevitably problematic business of people living together in close proximity, expecting that they should be all in all to each other, and one might reasonably conclude that the odds against completing the course of marriage – whether on Grand National or donkey-derby scale – are considerably higher than the figures indicate. It is not only that marriage is susceptible to problems, it is an inherently problematic personal relationship and social institution.

MIRAGES IN MARRIAGE

An important part of the problematic nature of marriage is connected with the expectations it excites. Many commentators upon the modern scene of family life have observed that the myths we entertain about marriage, personally and collectively, constitute the largest single explanation for the high incidence of marital stress and breakdown which have been evident in recent years. Within marriage there are four particularly common mirages. False notions about romantic love, persisting happiness in marriage, equality between man and woman, and individual free choice, combine to create a set of illusions and expectations which are likely to be disappointed.

MARRIAGE AND ROMANTIC LOVE

There are problems in our culture which follow from marrying on the basis of being 'in love', that 'extraordinary hallucination' as it has been called. This inspired and passionate warping of perception in favour of the loved one is invoked as sufficient justification for overriding all normal constraints on behaviour. After all, we say 'all is fair in love and war'. The state of being 'in love' is one which conjures up a mistiness of vision and intensity of experience which simultaneously inflates self-regard and accentuates our vulnerability. It is a bitter-sweet experience, the stuff of comedy and tragedy. Like Romeo and Juliet, we believe that love can overcome all barriers of race, class and material circumstance. Spellbound, we are as capable as Titania of transforming a mule-headed Bottom into the object of our heart's desire. Haunted, we preserve images of what might have been with those we barely know, although few of us go as far as the fourteenth-century poet Francesco Petrarch, who, having been captured by the sight of a beautiful married lady at the tender age of twenty-two, subsequently wrote 366 poems in her honour.

The temporary psychosis (as Freud called it) of being in love, with its distorted perceptions and idealizations, depends on maintaining a certain distance from reality. Even the great poets of chivalrous times distinguished romantic love from bawdiness or the boredom of everyday living together. Being 'in love' is very different from the active process of loving. This less dramatic commitment to another person requires more hard work and perseverance, unsupported as it is by the spellbound distortions of reality which encompass those who are in love. The active lover is distinguished from the spellbound lover by a measure of dispassion and a commitment to another 'warts and all'. To be an active lover is to have survived disappointment and disillusion.

Despite the madness of being in love, most of us want the intoxication of the experience and believe it to be the basis of a good marriage. Yet, with time, most of us accept that the headiness of the first stages of a love relationship will be succeeded by the more ordinary business of getting along with another person and managing the routines of everyday life together. However, the prolonged business of sharing personal and physical space is inherently problematic. Conflict is inevitable. Despite acceptance 'in the head' of what marriage entails, there frequently lingers 'in the heart' a regret and disappointment at what can feel like the spice having gone out of a relationship. The departure of romance can be experienced as an absence. Even among those who married on the basis of companionship without ever having been in love (and especially among those for whom a platonic involvement offered a welcome bypass around the turbulence of being in love) there may be a sense of something missing, a longing for what has never been. Those who use the urgency and *frisson* of being in love as a yardstick by which the health of their marriage is measured are particularly vulnerable to being seduced out of marriage by an affair. The seeds of marital breakdown are then sown among the romantic illusions we perpetuate.

Where do these illusions come from? Are they created by soft-focus cinematography, or by advertising imagery, or by the novels of Barbara Cartland? Powerful as such images may be, they are not the whole story. They reflect and respond to an appeal which arises from within. While they may whet our appetite, they do not provide an explanation for why that appetite exists in the first place, or why it is more prominent in some people than others. To explore these questions requires some psychological understanding of what is going on when we fall in love and how that experience is connected to other love relations we have or have not had. These connections will be explored in subsequent chapters. Here it is sufficient to note the strength of our primitive drive to become fused with another, and to exist in the shadow of the idealized object of our love. This drive has a purpose, as does the temporary blindness of being in love. People have to believe that what they see happening to others will not happen to them if they are to make first base. Being 'in love' makes such a leap in the dark possible. So does expecting life after marriage to remain blissful.

THE MIRAGE OF MARRIED BLISS

A moment's reflection demonstrates what a variety of emotions is contained in the word happiness. It is sometimes described as an experience which has to be pursued, a pleasure-seeking hedonism which aims to satisfy all the senses we are capable of using. At the other extreme, it is used to indicate an emotion which comes without warning or conscious effort, as C. S. Lewis conveys in the title of his autobiographical book *Surprised by Joy*. This kind of feeling can only be known in contrast with the full range of human experience, including fear, pain and sorrow. In our relationships we sometimes use the word 'happiness' to describe calm and contentment, a sense of being at one with the world and at peace with oneself. At other times we use the same word to describe the excitement, life and vitality which can come from a vigorous exchange with another person.

All these emotions are signs of an active love life. Only indifference indicates the death of love. In our search for a soul mate with whom we can experience living and loving it is easy to be disillusioned by conflicts and low points in the relationship. These are sometimes disqualified from being part of the expectations of married life as we try to preserve an image of the married state as a lifelong blissful union. It is not uncommon to hear (especially elderly) couples say they have never exchanged a cross word in their lives! This surely demonstrates the selective powers of human memory, or, as Dr Johnson said, describing remarriage, 'the triumph of hope over experience'. In terms of the blinkering effects of our determination to see what we want to see in our commitments, his observation applies equally well to first marriages. It resonates with the stark realism of an octogenarian who, when asked at his sixtieth wedding anniversary about the secret of a successful marriage, replied, 'Frequent separations and a growing loss of hearing'!

The mirage of married bliss is sustained by freeze-frame images of marriage – snapshots capturing a moment in time – rather than moving pictures. If married life is expected to remain like the photographs in a wedding album, disappointments are inevitable. Moving pictures have the advantage of recording different moods and seasons and linking them together as a cyclical whole. Collectively, we tend to view marriage as the normal state in which people carry on their domestic lives. Even those not taken in by soft-focus advertising and media hype are likely to see the 'family' as consisting of two married parents with their dependent children. That is the image which first springs to mind. In fact, the number of households in Britain which correspond with that image at any one time amounts to only around two-fifths of the total. And this is lower than the proportion of over a half thirty years ago. With one in five households with dependent children being headed by a lone parent, and more than one in three marriages being remarriages for one or both partners, you might say that our image of 'normal' family life is due for an overhaul. And you would be justified, even without taking into consideration a growing elderly population and the fact that we live in a cosmopolitan society accommodating many cultural and ethnic variations.

Yet most of us enter marriage refusing to recognize important differences. We tend to be friendly only with other couples once we ourselves are part of a couple. We become anxious if years pass and we have produced no children. We view second and subsequent marriages as if they were the same as first marriages, despite the fact that step-relationships interweave generations of adults and children in ways for which we have as yet devised no adequate terminology. Our images prove to be out of step with experience, and this in itself may provide some explanation of why, for example, remarriages are more vulnerable than first marriages.

The freeze-frame mentality can dominate individual as well as collective thinking. For young people, marriage represents an important step into adulthood. While restricted employment opportunities and the high cost of accommodation block other routes to the adult world, marriage may be a particularly attractive step to take. But for these same reasons young people may well postpone the decision to marry until they are in a position to afford it. Marriage is no longer a precondition for being sexually active; but for many it is still part of the process of leaving home and establishing an independent existence. For women in particular, marriage and motherhood continue to beckon attractively as solutions to the fundamental questions of life: Who am I? Where do I belong? What am I here for? At one extreme, the wedding can come to be regarded as the point of arrival, and not a point of departure. But marriages are not ready-made, and many marital problems are not simply the product of having chosen badly.

The mirage of marriage as the answer to life's problems creates its own pitfalls, especially for the young. These marriages are particularly prone to breaking down. In Britain the divorce rate for women married in their teens is twice as high as for those married between 20 and 24, and three times as high as for those marrying between 25 and 29. Particularly at risk are those who combine parenthood with marriage in their bid to leave home. Partnerships and parenthood entail commitments which may be in conflict with the adolescent yearning for release from the constrictions of family life. The experience of some young couples is that by marrying (and, perhaps, by starting a family too) they have jumped from the frying-pan of childhood into the fires of middle age, missing out on their single adulthood by exchanging one tie for another. Later, they may come to believe that in order to 'arrive' as individuals they must leave the marriage. Leaving home then becomes equated with leaving a partner who may have come to assume all the properties of a restrictive parent.

Expecting to enjoy lifelong married bliss is a tall order when 'until death do us part' can mean the next sixty years. We live at a time when elderly relatives far outnumber dependent children, a very different picture from the 1640s when the Englishman's expectation of life at birth was thirty-two years. At that time less than half of all marriages survived more than two years after the children had left home. The remarriage rate of 25 per cent was not far below the 36 per cent of today. The difference was that those marriages were broken by death and not by divorce. Even 150 years ago, 30 per cent of marriages were broken within fifteen years by the death of one partner. While longevity does not provide an adequate explanation of present divorce rates (because many marriages break down in the early years), it does affect the length of the commitment couples are being asked to make when they marry, and perhaps the expectations which have to be sustained to help them over that threshold. For women, who, as opposed to men, tend to care for the wider family, it may add to the pressures they have to face. Once the children have left home there may be elderly relatives to be looked after.

THE ILLUSION OF EQUALITY

One very significant aspect of our recent history has been the attention paid to the imbalance in the relations between men and women. The affluence of the post-war years has created employment opportunities which have resulted in some measure of economic independence for women. Economic independence creates choice. Choice has reshaped traditional assumptions about the roles men and women play. Women expect to be employed before marriage, and now the majority return to employment during or after the child-rearing years. Today, well over 60 per cent of married women in this country were in paid employment (as compared with one fifth in the 1950s), although the work is often poorly paid, of low status and part-time; the number of full-time jobs for women and men is steadily reducing. Nevertheless these changes have created a flurry of excitement, and in the 1970s there was talk of the emergence of the symmetrical family where both men and women had a working role inside and outside the home.[4] An expectation of equality between men and women has been created, one which is reinforced by legislation discouraging employers from discriminating against women when advertising for staff, and requiring them to hold jobs open during a period of maternity absence. This egalitarian ideal is readily transferred into expectations of marriage, expectations which can easily be disappointed when the ideology is in advance of what actually happens in practice.

An American sociologist, Jessie Barnard, was first to point out that men and women have different experiences of marriage.[5] These marriages within marriage have different trajectories, different satisfactions and different frustrations. She argued that women have the worst deal, and her position is supported by research which suggests that in terms of an individual's emotional and physical health, marriage offers more to men than to women.

One problem has been that while it is possible for men and women to contract an equal partnership in marriage while they have only themselves to consider, the situation changes radically when there are children. Marriage and parenthood are two distinct institutions, and parenthood works to reassert traditional divisions of labour between the sexes. Before marriage, the old divisions which required men to be sexually experienced and women to be virgins have almost disappeared. After marriage and before parenthood the assumption that men and women will both be in paid employment is reflected in the 'Dinky' (double income no kids yet) language of the workplace. But after parenthood his and her paths diverge. She usually attends to the children, remembers family birthdays and looks after his ageing relatives as well as her own. He attends to his job and his circle of (primarily male) friends. Should the marriage break, she is likely to find herself in poverty and he is likely to find himself without family. Half the fathers who divorce lose contact with their children within two or three years. Disconnected from family, it is small wonder that men remarry twice as frequently as women.

Why is it that children upset our egalitarian aspirations? One obvious effect of pregnancy is that it highlights an irreducible difference between men and women. Only women can have babies. Differences generate feelings – of admiration and envy, of love and hate, of veneration and contempt, of superiority and inferiority, of power and powerlessness. If equality is interpreted by partners as being exactly the same as each other, differences introduced by children will have a destabilizing effect on their relationship. Differences can no longer be denied when there are children. Parenthood also introduces a generation gap. Whereas a couple may draw comfort from being of the same generation, perhaps emphasizing the differences between themselves and their parents' generation, parenthood introduces generational differences into marriage. She is a mother as well as a wife; he is a father as well as a husband. As these roles are introduced, so perceptions change.

It has been argued that a society in which parenting has become the almost exclusive preserve of mothers has something to fear from women. As infants we are totally dependent upon the person who takes primary responsibility for looking after us. She is the person towards whom we experience our most intense and primitive emotions. She is also the person from whom we must grow apart. To enter the world of manhood, men have a longer psychological journey to make than women to establish a separate and acceptable identity for themselves. To compensate for this painful separation, and to afford protection against the primordial mother who has been so intensely loved and feared by males and females alike, society, it has been said, is organized in such a way as to give men prior claims to power, influence and authority. Here is a psychological perspective to put alongside economic and social explanations for the patriarchal society. It is one which sees shared parenting as the key to more equal relations than in the past between the men and women of future generations.

As things stand, men are likely to immerse themselves in their employment once there are children, not only because the financial burden of the family rests on their shoulders alone but also because they feel themselves to be displaced persons in their own homes. No longer can they call their wives their own. Women shoulder the brunt of domestic responsibilities which lack the status of their previous work. In doing so they sometimes lose the support they need from their husbands. In the pre-school years satisfaction from marriage can plummet to an all-time low, especially for women, a proportion of whom become chronically depressed. The drive to return to work is often as much to relieve social isolation and a sense of personal disintegration as it is to earn money. When women do return to work there is no guarantee that domestic responsibilities will be reallocated to take account of this change in role. Perversely, if a man should lose his job, his wife may give up her own job in order not to add to the damage already inflicted on his self-esteem by unemployment. In any event, if there is a conflict over whose job comes first, it is unusual for the woman to have prior claim.

The different seasons of men's and women's lives are not always in rhythm. The fact that men and women retire from their main occupation in life at different times is one point of difference and potential conflict. He may want to return home to her company when she is beginning to feel sufficiently free of the home to develop her own life, one which in all probability will last longer than his. The more he feels his powers and aspirations are being sapped by age and the challenges of younger men, the greater may be the temptation to dream of how the marriage once was before the children arrived. He may resent her growing participation in life outside the home and experience a crisis of identity that she had ten or fifteen years earlier when the children left home. His increasing claims on her may breed resentment in her, as if he were waiting to slam shut the cage door in her face. If he becomes ill or disabled she may feel cheated of a life for herself, yet unable to protest.

But the picture is not always like that. Many partners are happy to complement each other in marriage and find pleasure and satisfaction in doing so. In later life roles may be reversed, she developing a career of interests outside the home once the children have grown up, he taking early retirement to enjoy the fruits of his labours. They are able to handle competing claims on them as individuals and as partners in the marriage. But for this to happen, sufficient personal flexibility is required. In addition, there is a need for flexibility in our social and economic structures to enable men and women to move in and out of the many and varied roles they have the ability to play in their lives.

THE ILLUSION OF CHOICE

The struggle to achieve a better balance in the relations between men and women in marriage and in society at large has resulted from dissatisfaction with work being divided on an inside/outside basis. She works 'inside' the home, married to the house, devoted to the children and servicing the needs of her husband. He works 'outside' the home, bringing back a wage and providing a link with the world beyond the street where they live. She also works 'inside' in the sense that she is expected to be the intuitive, feeling partner in the relationship, the one in touch with subjective realities. He is expected to work 'outside' in the sense of being the productive side of the partnership, the instrumental doer. A study conducted in the 1950s in Britain, and repeated twenty years later,[6] suggests there has been some change in the basis of what makes for a good marriage. Where she used to want a breadwinner and he a good mother, cook and housewife, both now want a companion who is socially, intellectually and sexually compatible. If Freud encouraged the view that home and work lives were separate in his formula for a fulfilling life (*lieben und arbeiten*, to love and to work), today the goal is to rephrase the formula to read *Arbeit lieben*, to love work, whether that work is of an inside or outside nature.

In theory, this loosening of traditional divisions between the work of men and women increases choice. Neither sex has to conform to a stereotype that existed thirty years ago. Personally defined choices can take preference over social convention. The growing tendency for couples to cohabit can be seen as a sign of increasing privacy in determining how to live one's life. In an age of individualism a premium is placed on free choice. Social and geographical mobility encourages the view that 'the world is your oyster'. No longer do

19

people have the same compulsion to believe that out there in the great wide world is waiting the one person who is 'the intended'. Instead we say, 'There are plenty of fish in the sea.' In fantasy, the sky is the limit to the number of potential partners who will be good company, sexually compatible, share our interests, support our views and encourage our endeavours however ludicrous they may be.

These are high expectations to live up to. Elizabeth Bott, a social anthropologist, described our burdened partnership of today as 'the pressure-cooker marriage'.[7] Comparing the situation in western countries with those of less complex societies, she commented upon the many different roles partners have to perform for each other in modern marriages. Unlike couples in other cultures, where the extended family remains strong, western couples tend to go it alone. The privacy places additional burdens on our intimate relationships. Marriage has to provide more for the partners at a time when it is being supported less by society.

As public life becomes ever more complicated and demanding, it is not surprising that home life should be expected to provide a private haven. There the freedom to be and to express feelings and views uninhibited by social stricture is at a premium. Marriage can be seen as a refuge from the depersonalizing effects of a technological environment, a place where the rights of the individual may be emphasized to compensate for the demands and duties of the workplace. But because there are conflicting pulls between rights and duties, supports and demands, at home as well as at work, this illusion will generate its own conflicts.

Because we cannot make sense of experience in isolation, because we need to confirm and modify our perceptions, we rely upon our close relationships with others to help us fashion our identities. Individual and joint life histories are constructed, reworked and created through the continuous exchanges which take place between partners at different stages in their relationships. Courtship is a period, *par excellence*, where confidences are exchanged and identities negotiated. We tell our secrets in the hope of finding acceptance in the eyes of someone we love. By linking what has been with what is to come we give meaning to life. This process is intensified during periods of stress when established meanings may be called into question. At these times, the illusion of having free choice may generate anxiety and result in couples constantly examining what is happening in their relationship to see whether it is right for them. At worst, the effect can be similar to repeatedly digging up a young sapling for reassurance that the roots are healthy. At best, the experience can be liberating and enlivening.

Freedom to choose and the personal accountability that goes with it may become onerous burdens when there are few dependable social guidelines. Exercising choice can be a demanding business. Choosing whether and when to marry, where to live and work, how much contact to have with in-laws, whether and when to have children, how to divide domestic and parenting responsibilities, are decisions which take effort. But some choices are illusory. Natural endowments, local circumstances, the demands of family life and the consequences of past experience all restrict our freedom to choose the direction in which we would like to go. So often life becomes, in the words of John Lennon, 'what happens to you when you're planning other things'. The pressures of a rapidly changing social environment, combined with the different personalities and life experiences of the parties to marriage, ensure that freedom of choice is curbed. While partners may establish in their marriage a bolt-hole from the unfriendly world outside, they will encounter within some of the restrictions from which they seek to escape. Equally, those who need to turn outside the family to escape the confinements of intimacy have now to reckon with AIDS along with other checks and balances.

And what a relief these restrictions can be. The more uncertainty there is, the greater the pressure for guidelines and boundaries. Paradoxically, the absence of restrictions restricts freedom. There can be no game of football when the goalposts keep moving; there is no freedom to drive without an understanding about which side of the road to use. For most of us, the pressure to conform is strong. We want to know our experience is comparable with that of others, and this is especially true when things go wrong. The booming sales of books and magazines giving advice on personal problems, and the growth of radio and television programmes offering an array of experiences and points of view, are evidence of a hunger for an outside reference point to manage the choices involved in the business of modern everyday living.

THE PARADOX OF PARTNERSHIP

At different points in history marriage has swung pendulum-like between the poles of public and private concern. In eleventh-century Britain marriage was regarded as an entirely private arrangement; dissolution was a matter concerning no one but the parties to the contract. One hundred and fifty years ago divorce was a state concern and an Act of Parliament was required to bring a marriage to an end. In the turbulent 1990s we find ourselves somewhere between these extremes.

In writing about marriage as we see it today, and four illusions within the marriage mirage, we have touched on the personal and social aspects of the relationship and institution and briefly placed them in their economic and historical context. In any couple's relationship, the public world of collective responsibility meets the private world of individual rights. Janus-like, marriage faces both backwards and forwards in time, recapturing the past within an intimate present, and going on to forge the mettle of the next generation. It provides a focal point for many of the aspirations and dissatisfactions we experience in life. Differences of gender, culture, resources and experiences may be mediated within it.

Because marriage sits on the crossroads of so many aspects of life, the scope for conflict is broad. Like a mirror, marriage breakdown reflects a mixture of personal and social issues which are unresolved. Many of these issues have their roots in fear of intimacy, the problem of managing relations between men and women, the envy by the one sex of the other, the illusion about the nature of love and attainable happiness, and expectations of marriage and life generally. Often we do not know about our expectations until they are disappointed and we realize that something we had hoped for is missing. Disillusioned, we may precipitate a crisis or be tipped into one.

But just as the scope for conflict is so broad in marriage, so, too, is the room for personal development. At the heart of marriage lies a central paradox. In order to develop as individuals and be autonomous, people have to be involved with each other. Without an active interchange with others there is no possibility of learning about oneself. Without self-knowledge, relationships are likely to be impoverished and difficult to sustain. A desire to be involved with others is counterbalanced by a fear of being swamped or taken over by them. The more fragile the sense of self, the greater the fear of being defined from the outside. Yet without contact with the outside the inside atrophies. Throughout life, relationships are conducted on the basis of negotiating an acceptable boundary between those involved. There is a constant dance in which people move towards and away from each other. Without firm boundaries there can be no satisfying exchange; without permeability relationships become untenable. In marriage the paradox is neatly summed up in the phrase 'one flesh, separate persons'. Couples who manage the paradox are both separate in their togetherness and together in their separateness.[8]

Healthy relationships are those in which partners feel confident both about accepting each other as they are and pressing vigorously for change when this is necessary. Healthy individuals are those who can both stand their ground *and* be flexible. Healthy marriages are those where couples communicate openly about issues and feelings they want discussed without fearing they will hurt or be unduly hurt in the process. Healthy families are those in which the differences between members are respected, including the differences of hierarchy and generation. It is a brave man or woman who can claim full health in these terms. Indeed, it is almost a part of the human condition that we so frequently mis-manage our relationships and in that sense are so unhealthy a species.

Yet the drive to repair and integrate is strong. There is not only a biological drive to be paired to reproduce the species but a corresponding psychological drive to be attached for purposes of security and emotional fulfilment. In marriage there lie opportunities to repair previously damaged experiences of intimacy. The psychological drive to pair is reinforced and channelled by social pressures, although in which directions is not always easy to predict.

In psychological terms the task of marriage is to develop the capacity of people to relate to each other in a fulfilling way, not that marriage will necessarily succeed in this task. It requires a continuous, conscious effort from partners to recognize themselves and their spouses not only as the people they actually are, but also as the people they are in the process of becoming.[9] It implies a capacity to accept, love and forgive oneself as well as to accept, love and forgive one's partner. This is a tall order. It involves the attempt to convert what is often an unconscious element in the choice of partner into conscious commitment.

Many people do modify their original expectations of themselves and each other, achieve some of their hopes, manage their disappointments, grow up, handle conflict in their lives, adapt to the changing circumstances of family life and secure sufficient satisfaction to keep them married in a living and loving relationship. Surprising as it may seem, many of them also enjoy it and are enriched by it. To love and be loved so that, despite failings, each is the most precious person in the world to the other, even after forty or fifty years, can be one of the highest of human achievements and the greatest of satisfactions. Marriage then matters most importantly because it is a statement that we, as individuals, matter.

2. *Blueprints*

AN INFINITE VARIETY

When people talk together about marriage they often assume they are discussing the same thing. Women walking their children to and from school will talk of the trials and tribulations of married life as part of their everyday conversation. Men propping up the bar over lunch will bewail the loss of earlier freedoms when they were footloose and fancy free. Marriage will often be discussed with a kind of tolerant resignation as one of those burdens which have to be carried in life, the stuff of music-hall jokes: 'Since I've had my wife behind me I've never looked back!' And these casual conversations do not express a wish for anything to be different. They act as a bond between people through providing amusement or an experience shared and believed to be held in common. Frequently they are designed to suppress the different experiences people have of marriage. To complain seriously about a partner, or even to wax eloquent, would be to break the rules of the game and to cause embarrassment.

In public debate marriage can take on a political significance as its supporters and opponents do battle over whether or not it is good for men, good for women and good for society. In the heat of debate, when one side may accuse the other of not knowing what they are talking about, both sides will still assume they are talking about the same thing. Even when the argument is over the impossibility of generalizing about marriage, an image remains strong, to be supported or dismantled.

It is when individual experiences of marriage come under scrutiny that differences emerge most strongly. Most people consider themselves experts on marriage on the basis of their own experience. And, in the ordinary course of events, everyone is reluctant to accept that others have an expertise which is relevant to their personal situation. People tend to believe, and sometimes fear, that their predicament is highly individual. And this is both true and untrue. 'All cases are unique, and very similar to others,' declares Reilly about marriage in T. S. Eliot's *The Cocktail Party*. 'All happy families are alike but an unhappy family is unhappy after its own fashion,' observes Leo Tolstoy in the opening lines of *Anna Karenina*. Only when things go wrong is the veil of privacy which normally conceals the workings of married life lifted, and usually in the hope of discovering that what is happening in one marriage is not, after all, so dissimilar from what is happening in others.

In the last chapter we looked at how the social institution of marriage has changed at different times in history. We also looked at the diversity of living arrangements which operate between couples today, even before account is taken of our ethnically diverse, multi-cultural society. Why do we continue to talk about marriage as if it were a commonly understood state when these differences so obviously exist? Where do we learn how to behave in the intimacy of marriage? Who teaches us what it means to be a man or a woman? What are the primary influences upon our development as sexual beings?

None of these questions can be satisfactorily answered without taking account of individual histories. History is an amalgam of fact and fiction. It consists of verifiable events which took place in the past and the stories people tell each other to explain how they come to be where they are. Everyone needs their own story. Without an account of where we come from we cannot know who we are. Until we know who we are we are not free to become fully involved with others.

Strange as it may seem, history is often discounted when marriage is threatened by crisis. An unhappy marriage is more likely to be explained in terms of current stresses than in relation to what has gone on long before. However, current stresses provide important but insufficient explanations of marital crises. Some people are capable of weathering the most horrendous adversities and catastrophes and coming through relatively unscathed by their experiences. Others sink in what outsiders might regard as a storm in a teacup. It is not so much what happens to people that is important as what they think has happened to them. It is less the events which matter than the interpretation placed on those events. And the framework people use to make sense of their experiences is developed over time and so has strong connections with the past.

What complicates this state of affairs is that none of us has perfect recall of the past. About the earliest years, when we are most impressionable, none of us has a conscious memory. The blueprints we draw up about the environment we inhabit and our place in it are sketched in outline when we are very young and least able to see the whole picture. The process of modifying these bold early sketches so that they match experience takes a lifetime. Even so, most modifications take place in childhood. Conscious learning is only a small part of the process. Rather, we absorb what is going on around us, especially from those who are most intimately involved with us. We are most receptive during the tender, vulnerable years, the years which we have most difficulty in recalling. Although this book is about marriage, this chapter needs to take the reader back into history because therein lie our roots and forgotten history has a tendency to be relived.

FORGOTTEN HISTORY

Take the case of John Ladbroke. John Ladbroke married late. Through his twenties and early thirties he had a succession of short-lived relationships with girlfriends which usually ended when they tired of his unreliable and generally difficult behaviour. At the age of thirty-four he met and married within a very short space of time a widow who was four years his senior. She had a young boy by her first marriage. While he was courting her, John was very protective towards mother and son, and acted like a big daddy to them both. One year into marriage he became irritable, demanding and critical, much as he had been in earlier relationships.

John was an only child whose mother had died when he was at the difficult and demanding age of toddlerhood. His father employed a succession of nannies, who always left just when he was beginning to get used to them. At the age of seven, he was sent away to boarding-school and this event more or less coincided with his father's remarriage. The first seven years of his life, then, were peppered with separations. How was he to interpret these events? What effects might they have on his self-image? What kind of predictions would he be likely to make about the behaviour of those he became involved with?

Perhaps not surprisingly, he was cautious in later life about committing himself in his relationship with others. He alienated those he feared were becoming too important to him, and they rejected him in the manner to which he had become accustomed. His wife and his son, however, struck a different chord. Maybe because of their bereavement, John felt a special bond of understanding with them. Not that he could have put this into words. He would just say that they evoked a great warmth in him. This warmth was sufficient to help him over the threshold of marriage. But one year later he was behaving towards his wife in the way he had treated, and tested, the other women in his life.

On the face of it, his wife, Jean, had a very different formative experience. She came from a large family of seven children, of whom she was the eldest. She would recall the boisterous rough and tumble of her younger brothers playing and fighting with each other in a tolerant but resigned way, rather like a mother talking about her unruly offspring. And in some ways that was the position she had occupied in her family. Her parents both went out to work, and from a young age Jean had been given the responsibility of looking after the other children. In some ways she had enjoyed her position. It gave her a special place in her mother's eyes. All this had changed when she was thirteen and her five-year-old sister had died of a sudden illness.

Jean's precocious bubble of confidence, which had earned her the attention of her parents, was replaced by a sense of guilt about what had happened which lasted into later life. She was reserved in her adult relationships, reluctant to make claims on others and inhibited from offering what she had to give. When her husband died she became withdrawn. John succeeded in breaking through this envelope of privacy. His line of chat, and a *bonhomie* which could at times border on insensitivity, marked him out for her as a survivor; someone with whom she could risk herself; someone who could both carry and withstand her. As she allowed herself to close the gap in their relationship, John became irritable and demanding. She felt at one level that this was no worse than she deserved. At another she was deeply resentful.

The most basic of all human drives is directed towards forming and sustaining attachments to others. For the new-born baby, the balance between life and death depends upon the success of this enterprise. Hunger, pain, fatigue and illness all require attention if the baby is to thrive. But attachment is more than cupboard love. Parents are needed to respond to the overtures of their offspring, to stimulate their interest and to provide a living presence to which they can relate. Everything the young baby does is designed to interest and attract the attention of others, especially those who are in closest proximity. The prolonged crying of a well-fed and recently changed baby cannot be ignored, however hard the parents may try to develop an impervious barrier against what might seem an unremitting demand. The gurgling noises and toothless smiles are enough to melt the resolve of the most hard-pressed mothers. Rather like the proverbial granny in the attic, the baby in the nursery is usually capable of summoning an immediate response to his imperious demands.

Babies are, of course, very different from each other right from the start. They come into the world not just as bundles of flesh and bone but with already distinctive personalities capable of initiating different responses from those around them. They are not lumps of clay awaiting the potter's wheel of their parents' influence to fashion their personalities, but equal partners in taking initiatives and creating contretemps.

Unlike baby goslings which lock on to the first moving object in sight, the newborn baby will be relatively undiscriminating about who tends his needs for the first three or four months of life. He will be content to be passed around a circle of admiring adults as if he were a parcel. But thereafter, and certainly by the time he is six or seven months old, he will have developed a definite preference for the person who has a particular responsibility for him.

The attachment to a preferred person develops most strongly in the first year of life. In our culture, mothers are most likely to occupy this favoured position. Women suckle and tend the physical needs of their young, and are available to play with them and respond to them. It is through these interactions that babies come to recognize the distinctive sight, smell and manner of their mother. From eight months onwards they are likely to protest loudly about being passed around, and cling to the person they know best. Although they may develop attachments to several people, one person will be preferred. But from the age of a year onwards it becomes increasingly difficult for this preferred attachment to form because the infant's behaviour is then also governed by a fear of the unfamiliar. When an attachment has been formed, there is a person the baby can turn to in threatening situations. When no such bond exists, the position is more complicated.

With time, and the development of physical and mental abilities, babies are able to make their first moves towards independence. They learn to crawl and then to walk, and the first direction in which they are likely to move is away. They develop the rudiments of adult language, and the word they will use most frequently (after 'Mummy' and 'Daddy') is 'No'. These exploratory adventures are conducted in the safe knowledge that they are carried out within sight of a parent, and if there is ever any doubt about this the infant can throw the occasional backward glance for reassurance.

During the first three years of life the young child will venture out from and return to the secure base of a parent's presence when conducting expeditions into unfamiliar territory. The secure knowledge of a parent's presence is the precondition for such exploration, as it is for satisfying curiosity and for sharing new experiences. Through repeated encounters with different people and different objects, the child becomes capable of making predictions about how others will behave, and learns that actions have consequences. Very gradually, the secure base that the mother provided 'out there' becomes absorbed and assimilated within the young child so that she is 'in here' and does not always have to be kept in sight.

This sense of security, derived from developing a basic trust in the people most closely involved in their upbringing, provides the fundamental outline of the personal blueprints children draw on to guide them successfully through the relationships they form in later life. Without reliable guidelines there is no sense of safety in the unpredictable business of forming new relationships. Secure attachments early on in life provide inner resources to manage stressful and threatening situations in later years. John Bowlby, the man who pioneered what has become known as 'attachment theory',[1] drew a military analogy to underline the importance of establishing and maintaining a secure base in handling unfamiliar and threatening situations:

> The safety of an army in the field is dependent not only on defending itself against direct attack but also on its maintaining open communications with its base . . . we should be as much concerned with threats to the rear as with threats to the front.

Threats to the rear occur throughout life, although with less frequency and intensity than during childhood. But the ordinary events of life – illness, bereavement, infirmity – all heighten our urge to behave in ways which echo our childhood needs. Then we are likely to seek out people who can be close to us, sometimes clinging to them for support, as if our own security was dependent upon their actual and continued physical presence.

What happens if the conditions for establishing basic trust and security are unfavourable during the early years of childhood? How do young children react to that situation? What will be the consequences in later life? In the 1950s some very powerful films were made about the reactions of children to separation from their parents when admitted to hospital or residential nurseries.[2] These films, combined with Bowlby's work, made a significant impact on hospital policy, discouraging the separation of sick children from their parents. The films highlighted three phases of separation reactions.

First of all, children were likely to protest about their parents' departure. They would show signs of acute distress, crying loudly and vigorously. This attempt to call their parents back could last for hours, days, even for a week or more. When this protest failed, despair would follow. The children remained preoccupied by their loss and would continue to cry from time to time, but in an increasingly hopeless and dejected way. They would tend to withdraw from their surroundings, showing little interest in those around them and making few demands upon them. Finally came a state of detachment which could misleadingly be regarded as recovery. Children would appear to adapt, would resume an interest in their toys, recover their appetite and smile at the staff. But there was a detachment in their manner which shut people out, and frequently these children would refuse to take any notice of their parents when they came to visit. The longer the period of separation, the more unfamiliar the environment, the more frequent the change of people offering alternative care and attention, and the more discomfort the child was in, the greater the trauma of the separation. The experience was likely to be most harmful between six months and three years of age. To compensate for their losses, children were likely to retreat into a private world and to form attachments to inanimate objects which were more securely under their control.

The fear of being on one's own applies beyond childhood, and for good reasons. Individuals who are isolated are vulnerable. We do not have to fear predators in the same way as do other animals, but because we are social beings and rely upon others for survival, learning and fulfilment in life, company is essential. A basis of secure attachment enables people not only to get on with others but also to achieve a measure of autonomy in their lives. And as Bowlby points out, autonomy does not supersede the need for close relationships as adults:

> Paradoxically, the truly self-reliant person . . . proves to be by no means as independent as cultural stereotypes suppose. An essential ingredient is a capacity to rely trustingly on others when occasion demands, and to know on whom it is appropriate to rely.[3]

What relevance has the concept of attachment to the predicament John and Jean Ladbroke found themselves in?

We might surmise that the separations John experienced between the ages of two and seven years resulted in the development of an internal blueprint predicting that close relationships were unlikely to be sustained, and cautioning against becoming involved with others. Rather than contend with the pain of being left, he ensured that relationships broke down if they were in danger of becoming important to him. Or the situation could be read another way. With those who reached him emotionally he recreated the rejections he had experienced as a young child.

To what end, you might ask? Later on we shall be suggesting that some conflicts in marriage can be seen as an attempt to put right experiences which have gone wrong in the past. For now it is sufficient to assert that John, having loved and lost, felt he would be tempting providence to allow himself to love again. The blueprint based on his earlier experiences ensured that the old drama was played out time and time again, thereby validating its own predictions. In toddler terms, it was as if he confirmed the pattern etched in his mind that the part of him which needed to be loved exclusively, and which could throw tantrums if this need was thwarted, was simply not acceptable to others. His success in summoning up the devil he knew blinded him to any awareness of his own part in bringing about the final outcome. Only through his marriage, which for him was unconsciously rooted in an identification with the bereaved, did he create the conditions where it became more difficult to drive out or cut off from the attachment he both yearned for and feared. Through marriage he created the possibility of consciously knowing about and coming to terms with his own painful experience of loss.

And the same was true for Jean. Behind the little girl who was so good at looking after others was another little girl longing to be looked after herself. Part of her motivation in caring for her younger brothers and sister was the wish to earn a special place in her parents' affection. There would always have been ambivalence towards her charges because they were not only a means to an end, but also rivals for the limited rations of parental attention. Jean's reaction to her sister's death was complicated by this fact.

The death of a husband would almost certainly have resurrected for Jean the complicated feelings associated with her earlier bereavement. Against the odds John succeeded in drawing her out of a withdrawn reaction. He did not have to fear being overwhelmed by this recluse; she did not have to fear his vulnerability. She was drawn towards the resilience of a man who offered the possibility of providing something which had eluded her during childhood – the exclusive love of a parent. But perhaps she also identified in John the orphan she half recognized herself to be. Their relationship offered a prospect of changing the blueprints drawn up by history.

Neither would consciously have recognized or construed their position in this way. As far as John was concerned women were untrustworthy and unpredictable. And because Jean, quite irrationally, felt partly responsible for her sister's death, that hypothesis fitted both their internal blueprints at some level. No one amends lightly something as vital as a blueprint. Moreover, they would have been unlikely to make any connection between what was happening in their adult relationships and what had happened during childhood. In this they are not alone. While it is self-evident that childhood experiences must have a profound formative effect upon the beliefs we have about ourselves and upon our expectations of others, most of us fail to take them into account when we run into trouble later on in life. Nowhere is this amnesia more likely to apply than within the intimacy of marriage.

THE DAWN OF CONSCIOUSNESS

So far we have considered the significance of attachment in relation to the fundamental but rather general issue of whether it is safe to rely upon others at all. Establishing a degree of basic trust is a key foundation-stone upon which subsequent social development can build. But development does not stop there. There are many aspects of childhood which are affected by experience, and these change with time. Parents are more responsive to some characteristics of their children than to others, and also to some stages of their development than to others.

The early years of life are intensely physical years. Parents feed their babies, cuddle them, change their nappies, smooth cream on their bottoms, bath them, tickle them and generally communicate through bodily involvement. If they do not feel easy about this physical closeness that, too, will form part of the communication. Parents may hold their babies close and convey love for and admiration of their bodies, or they may hold them away and register distaste, even disgust, for some of their bodily functions. In the early stages, the baby's mouth is an important point of contact with the world. At first the world consists of the breast, then it extends to include the mother, and then other people and objects. Oral satisfactions die hard. Adults eat to excess to ease depression, turn to the bottle for comfort or suck contentedly on a pipe. These are not baby habits, but they are habits which have a link with babyhood experiences.

As children grow older they will become more consciously aware of the likes and dislikes of those who care for them. They will be eager to perform and so please parents who are appreciative of their efforts and admiring of what they produce from inside themselves. They will give in the confident expectation that their gift will be well received. They may behave differently towards parents who seem repelled by their efforts, and in learning to control may also learn to withhold. As food can become the ammunition in a battle of wills between children and their parents, so, too, can the process of toilet training. In adult life we talk about people withholding what they have in order to keep control; we talk about 'shitty' behaviour to describe what happens when someone 'messes things up'.

Sexual development is closely linked with body language and bodily contacts of early childhood. The way young children's bodies are handled, the way their bodily needs are attended to, and the physical ambience of this early intimacy prepare the ground for feelings encountered later in life, when genital maturity allows sexual expression to be added to the repertoire of ways of relating and communicating. Genital interest occurs early in childhood. Daddy's and brother's 'thing' and Mummy's and sister's 'bottom' command great interest at bathtime from children as young as two and three years of age. If observations and questions are not permitted, curiosity is stifled and frustrated. Equally, too much frankness and bodily display can cause children to shy away or feel uneasy. The atmosphere, whether it be one of confidence, inhibition or embarrassment, will contain a vital message for the child and leave its legacy in adult life.

In learning what is and is not acceptable to parents, children come to know when and how to harness their feelings and impulses, as well as how to control their bodily functions. In the process they are vigorously engaged in discovering what belongs to them and what belongs to others. Such distinctions are very difficult for the newborn baby, who has neither the experience nor the necessary mental and physical equipment. As far as we can tell, babies regard their mothers as an extension of themselves, yet not quite connected, rather like those fingers and toes which, although attached, are happened upon in surprise. They associate pleasure with the presence of mother and the fullness and satisfaction which follow sucking at her breast. Pain and frustration are frequently associated with her physical absence.

Those who have paid special attention to the interactions of parents and very young children say that the confusion between what belongs to self and what belongs to others applies with even more force to feelings than it does to bodies, and for very much longer. Frustrated and angry babies can cry themselves into a state of fear as they interpret the absence of their mother as an attack upon themselves. Their own anger with their mother for not being there is then attributed to her, and their fear results from believing she is in the rage that they themselves are in. Adults have strong feelings too, susceptible to those of children. There is something primitive about babies which can fill parents with intense feelings of love and hate. It is as if the emotional umbilicus is never cut, and so magical transfers of feeling remain possible. Such transfers are the basis of firm bonds and major misunderstandings.

The confusion between what belongs to me and what belongs to you (in emotional terms) goes on throughout life. The degree of confusion usually reduces with the passage of time, although it can be heightened at any point in life as a result of threat or adversity. How the unexperienced feelings of one person can be experienced by another is not an easy process to explain. Indeed, the process is unconscious in the sense that neither party is aware of what is taking place. Yet the phenomenon is familiar to us all, particularly when we discover we are responsible for something for which we had blamed others. It can happen towards objects as well as people. The man who kicks his car because it refuses to start (and he has not checked the petrol gauge) is not unlike the toddler who kicks the table for walking into him. The logic of the unconscious creates a free trade area for emotional trans- actions. Sometimes they are acted upon in violent terms; many atrocities are committed against innocents in the name of nationalism, religion or a personal crusade. More ordinarily, they form the stuff of everyday re- lationships as we blame or criticize others for doing or saying the things we feel inside ourselves.

What is common to all these situations is the process of separating out 'good' from 'bad'. This distinction is usually socially determined and given momentum by the basic need to be attached to others, particularly during the impressionable years of early childhood. In managing very strong desires and impulses the child has his relationship with his parents as a resource. Parents have the means of satisfying and frustrating the child's wishes, of gradually checking a tendency to monopolize their lives and of encouraging steps towards self-reliance. In this process, strong clashes of will are inevitable, but with luck parents and children will come out of the experience confident that their security is not jeopardized by conflict, and that seemingly unmanageable feelings and impulses can be harnessed and contained.

We depend upon others for this kind of social education throughout life.

We test our realities against those of others, and we modify them as we have to. This process of learning takes place more rapidly and intensely during the early years of childhood than in later life. For children, the world is one of extremes. The 'baddies' are firmly distinguished from the 'goodies'. They take the form of witches and fairies, beasts and beauties, villains and rescuers. The forces of good and evil are ranged against each other in a struggle for victory, and the future depends upon the triumph of good. 'Good' is the experience of feeling secure and fulfilled in a relationship; 'bad' is the converse. In this way children make the first crude distinctions between what is 'me' and what is 'not me'. Only later will they come to learn the shades of grey in which we are both what we would like and what we would prefer not to be. At this early stage, however, life seems to depend upon expelling from 'me' all that seems to be bad, and later testing out how far others will tolerate or react to the bad in 'me'.

Toddlers who kick and scream against the restrictions of their parents are unconsciously testing the limits of where they end and others begin. As far as they are concerned, of course, they are simply wanting another ice-cream, or another go on the swing. If they are over-indulged they will, as likely as not, feel unsatisfied. What they may unconsciously be looking for is containment. Containment relieves anxiety about strong feelings and impulses getting out of control. Instead of the children being the monsters, the parents become the monsters who threaten to take over and exact revenge. But if the monster parents do not act monstrously and succeed in containing the passion, the children are reassured. They do not have to protect themselves from the monster. They can even identify with it and incorporate it inside themselves in a less monstrous form. With the help of others they have then learned to manage their feelings and not to be afraid of them. Moreover, what they take back inside themselves is an experience of the relationship in which the monster was tamed. And this experience modifies earlier drafts of their personal blueprint of the social world.

Sometimes, however, the exchange does not have a reassuring outcome. Toddlers may succeed in eliciting a punitive response. Or they may fail to evoke a response at all. They are then left on their own to worry about the threats from within and without. They may redouble their efforts to provoke others to contain benignly what is bubbling up inside them or, if that fails, to secure punishment for being so bad. But if an alliance cannot be made with the parents against what feels uncontrollably bad inside them, they may defect and identify with the 'bad'. From time to time all children do this as part of the process of discovering themselves. Sometimes they fear that the strength of their passion will so endanger relationships which are important to them that they will shut down parts in themselves from which they believe the threat comes. This may buy some short-term security, but at the cost of limiting how much of themselves can be revealed and used in relationships with others. These self-imposed restrictions may not be limited to the negative emotions. The desire to love and be physically close may be repressed if it is seen to pose a threat. Indeed, the positive emotions are frequently more threatening than the negative ones because they open us up to others, and they allow us to become lost in causes greater than ourselves. Fusion, like separation, brings the fear of losing oneself.

Through play, and in the world of imagination and fantasy, children relive situations which both bring them pleasure and cause them anxiety.[4] Teddies are scolded, dolls nursed through illness and injury, play houses are constructed and play families arranged to live in them. On a good day (for the parents, that is) children can be absorbed for hours in the imaginative construction of a world which depends on them alone for its realization and reward. Through play children act out in miniature the adult dramas of life and learn how to master new situations. They also give expression to their feelings about situations which worry them and by doing so provide some relief from anxiety.

Throughout life, a capacity to play, to symbolize, and to have access to the world of fantasy can assist people to come to terms with life. Theatre, film, television and books can play a vital part in the process, providing a psychological service within our cultural heritage. Play can increase the extent to which people feel able to involve themselves with others and extend the parts of their personalities they can use. Material objects may become temporary substitutes for important relationships, like the mauled soft toy or ragged piece of blanket in childhood, but it is only when relationships with 'things' rather than people become an established pattern for 'shutting out' that there is cause for concern. It is only when the private world of fantasy becomes a hideaway from real relationships that our personally constructed blueprints fail to serve their proper purpose. Personality development is impaired when an individual has shut down a broad range of feelings and ways of relating, in the belief, unconsciously arrived at, that it is unsafe to do otherwise. Objects and fantasy are then used not as a means of venturing out, but to beat a retreat.

From the toing and froing of the social exchanges of the early years, exchanges which are imbued with misperception and misattribution, children construct blueprints of their world and their place in it. At the beginning of life the world is very small, and the infant's place in it very large. This balance changes with the passage of time as experience fashions these blueprints into more serviceable guides. They are like charts which allow predictions to be made about the likely consequences of taking different courses of action. Some parts of the blueprint will have been tried and tested, and found to be reliable. Others will be the product of guesswork because the terrain they cover is unknown, and being unknown will contain risks. Yet these backwaters of consciousness will have great influence upon the channels of communication which are regularly used in dealings with others in later life. To 'be at one with the world' requires a fit between the blueprints constructed internally and the behaviour of the world outside. When the two do not match up there is pressure either to revise the blueprints or to change the environment. This tension is the stimulus for social learning and personal development. There is constant pressure to bring 'insides' and 'outsides' into conjunction with each other. Whether the resolution is through modifying blueprints or coercing others to conform with our internal codes, providing there is sufficient basic trust and security to allow the two worlds to meet, a process of mutual influence will operate.

The intimate relationships we form in later life, among which marriage is arguably the most important, create opportunities for personal and social development to continue with renewed impetus. The physical and emotional intimacy of adult sexuality in marriage recreates aspects of our early, and often unremembered, pasts. The pleasures, anxieties and inhibitions associated with those earlier years frequently come back to haunt us, but in new guises and with different partners. John and Jean Ladbroke may find through their marriage that their feelings towards each other are connected with behaviour which resurrects childhood 'rejections' and 'damage'. Both stand to gain from working at some of the separate psychological burdens brought with them into marriage. Alternatively, they may prefer the limited protection provided by keeping each other (and their own needs) at arm's length by replaying the old scenarios. That at least confirms their predictions of how the world is. Either way, they have to face the possibility of discovering discrepancies between what they expect and what they experience, and in that lies the potential for development.

THIRD PERSONS

So far we have considered the development of marriage blueprints in a way which does not take account of sexual differences and which assumes that learning takes place in the context of a two-person relationship, principally between a child and one or other of his parents. Clearly, the process of development is more complex than that. As children become older they mix with more and more people, extending the range of their experience and modifying their blueprints in the process. Brothers, sisters, cousins, aunts, uncles, grandparents, friends and teachers, all contribute to widening the child's social world, and sometimes the significance of these people will be equal to if not greater than that of parents.

Despite there being many different forms of family life in Britain today, the great majority of children spend their early years with their two natural parents. This fact creates a triangular constellation of relationships with its own particular contribution to make to the process of development. What is the psychological significance for adult life of having two parents?

Although children can be attached to more than one person from a very early age, there is usually one parent who is special – even if only in the sense that their presence can be taken for granted. That relationship is regarded in proprietorial terms by young children who will feel threatened by and jealous of any claims made by others on the affections of their first and own love. Usually the special parent is mother. The problem comes when a child begins to recognize that another has claim upon her affections – father. What is the child to do? A colleague of ours described the reactions of her four-year-old son to the news that his mother was to have another baby. Climbing into his parents' bed one morning, and establishing himself firmly between them, he declared that when he grew up he was going to marry his mummy. 'And what about Daddy?' inquired his amused mother. 'Oh he'll be dead,' replied the boy, in a matter-of-fact way.

The tragedy of Oedipus Rex was given archetypal significance by Freud[5] when he claimed it encapsulated the universal unconscious wish of young boys to dispense with their fathers in order to establish an exclusive claim upon their mothers. The wish is based upon the child's knowledge that he has a rival. The idea that there is rivalry between fathers and sons for possession – even sexual possession – of father's mate is one which is neither readily digested nor easily given up. The 'Oedipus complex' has become part of our common language, and yet it is seldom taken seriously (except by parents of four-year-old boys – and even then it is unexpected).

Despite this reserve, the figure of Oedipus has made much more impact upon the theory of male development than has that of Electra upon female development. Not surprisingly, there has been reaction against the patriarchal notion that a woman is psychologically inferior and physically incomplete in not having a penis, although social realities have, and still do, provide grounds for envy of the male state, if not the male member. Because babies grow inside their mother, because she is usually the person to feed and physically care for them, and because she provides the emotional anchorage which makes exploration possible, she has enormous importance. She is the all-powerful source of satisfaction and frustration, happiness and sadness, love and hate. The fact that mothers are usually the first object of love for their offspring creates real differences between boys and girls when it comes to relinquishing that tie. It is here that fathers play an important part.

At first, the father's contribution (and we are here making the assumption that he is not the principal parent) does not have a differential impact on boys and on girls.[6] He acts to supplement the resources of mother. By being physically and emotionally available to her, and by relieving her of economic worries, he supports her labour of love. Of course, it does not always work out like that. The financial needs of the family, the demands of a career and the needs of a father in his own right directly affect his availability to his children and have an indirect effect through the support he can offer his partner. But mothers cannot parent in a social vacuum. The more isolated they are, the less they are able to act effectively as parents. Because the man continues his role outside the home he provides a window on the adult world which may be sorely needed by his partner when she fears she is slowly sinking beneath piles of dirty nappies and baby talk. He can also take over the parenting role and provide her with respite from the rigours of what is a twenty-four-hour-a-day job. By so doing he provides her with some immunity against the chronic depression which afflicts so many mothers of pre-school age children, and which in turn undermines their abilities as parents.

As children become older, fathers have a role to play in encouraging exploration and play. They provide opportunities for making relationships outside the confines of the early exclusive twosome. They are there to be hugged, fought and played with. Although it is true that some fathers are involved with their children for seconds in a day rather than hours or even minutes, their presence can encourage confidence to make those expeditions and explorations which are vital to the process of child development.

But there is another and more fundamental way in which fathers contribute towards the development of their children. Because they, too, have a special relationship with a child's mother – with its own areas of physical and emotional exclusivity – children have to give up the illusion that they own their mother, and so they must learn to share. They have to come to terms with the fact that there is a rival in the camp, a rival they would both love to remove but hate to lose because of his separate contributions to home life. In coming to terms with conflicting feelings about the relationship between their parents, and being helped to do so, children assimilate the capacity to manage other relationships in which they are not the centre of attention and from which they may be excluded. They are then impelled neither to intrude upon nor retreat from those who have other close relationships. In short, they learn to relate in a way which is inclusive rather than exclusive. They learn the difference between drawing a line in relationships which defines who can be involved in what, and the kind of rejection which requires a relationship to end.

The process of drawing a line, setting limits, establishing a boundary, is a vital part of social development. It is the basis for the blueprints which guide human behaviour. Parents draw the line between what takes place between them as partners (from which the children are excluded) and what takes place between them as parents with their children. These vital distinctions protect children from experiences which might compromise or abuse their childhood. When parents relate to their children as if they were partners and look to them for the support and even sexual comfort that should come from other adults, the boundary surrounding and protecting childhood is broken. The freedoms of childhood include flirting with father and attempting to seduce mother in the safe knowledge that this is play and it will not get out of hand. By this means children come to learn that their feelings can be expressed without fear of abuse, and their sexuality is both acceptable and manageable.

Children also witness their parents operating as a couple. From their direct observations they absorb a model of marriage. How intimate are couples in public? Is it safe for them to disagree or to argue? How separately do they operate? How together are they? These and many other unformulated questions are being answered each day by the way parents conduct their routines and lives together. Unknowingly, the most potent of all sex-education programmes is taking place; the ground is being laid for the partnerships of the next generation.

What is also taking place is the formation of sexual identity, the growing allegiance to male or female gender through identification with one or other parent. The young boy relinquishes his primary attachment to his mother in order to accompany father to the allotment, to the DIY store or on a fishing expedition. The bond which grows up between them is some compensation for giving up mother. Becoming a man in his father's mould offers the boy an identity for the future, and one that will receive encouragement from family friends and relatives. With time and proper encouragement he will become a man in his own right, determining his own direction, and relatively unaffected by trying to secure the approval and attention of his parents. But this will not always happen successfully. There is a cartoon which depicts a statue to an elder statesman bearing the inscription, 'An inspiration to his country, a leader of men, but still a disappointment to his mother'. Some present-day achievements are motivated by the hurt of being ignored in the past; they can represent an attempt to go backwards in time to recover early special relationships in the family. Success is then the cover concealing and even obliterating the real person inside under the mantle of a false self.

If there is no father, or father-substitute, in a family, it is likely to be boys who have the greatest difficulty in finding a secure identity. They have the greater journey to make when separating from their mothers.[7] Girls can continue to cultivate their links with their mothers throughout life. They share a common gender identity and many of the experiences and activities associated with it, even as these change and evolve over time. Boys will seldom be able or wish to preserve the degree of closeness to their mothers that it is open for girls to do. They must cross the gender divide to join their fathers, both to help them cope with the pain of parting from their first love and also to match social expectations of the male sex. The third person, in the shape of father, provides a worthy opponent, a vital stepping-stone and, with luck, a more than sufficient compensation.

THE SOCIAL FILTER

The basic and rather crude blueprints fashioned in the earliest years are tried and tested against social realities, first at home and later in the world outside. Brothers and sisters provide competition as well as a further reason for having to share and cooperate with others. Older children may look after new additions to the family and learn about being a parent by doing so. Or they may hope that their contribution to the household economy will restore them to a special place in their parents' affections. The impulse to partner parents can be as strong for children as the temptation for parents to confide in their children as if they were partners.

As the social world of children broadens to include school, friends, television and public heroes, so too does the range of influences which bear upon personal blueprints for living. With age, the sensitivity to external influence decreases, but there are critical points in the process of growing up when children are more than usually pliable. These are the in-between years when a crossing is being made between one phase of life and another. At school, teachers supply their pupils with examples of adult behaviour, which in many respects will supplement and sometimes take over from the models supplied by parents. Sports heroes and pop stars provide images for teenagers, who may imitate them and style themselves upon them. These models from the 'me' generation are frequently set up in opposition to the 'they' models of the parents' generation. They provide an alternative of extremes which help the half-child, half-adult teenager to find a place in the adult world without being a carbon copy of his parents. Rather as the soft toy or ragged piece of blanket provide transitional objects in early childhood, these figures provide transitional attachments, and reflections of an ideal self, which help the individual towards autonomy. Recognizing the influence of these figures, advertisers who wish to promote products in a youth market or to discourage drug abuse will summon up images of the alternative culture.

Part of the fantasy about adolescent heroes is that they are in perfect command of their situation and can control the events and people around them. Their attraction is based on an image which is at the other extreme from the uncertainty and powerlessness which are also part of adolescence. The young adult oscillates wildly between the extremes of omnipotence and impotence in a search for competence. During this period there will be pressures to woo and be wooed and to gain sexual experience. Personal uncertainty will combine with social pressure to encourage experiment. The nature of the experiment will, however, be directed more towards self-discovery and self-reassurance than towards relating to a real other person. Sexual experience is part of coming of age, breaking the seal of sexual mythology and entering into the adult world.

Adults will watch the sexual emergence of their offspring, or their friends' offspring, with a mixture of satisfaction, anxiety and envy. Depending upon the social circles in which the young adult moves there will be more or less pressure towards getting married. The better-off are likely to be advised to delay serious relationships until they have more life experience. The less well-to-do may encourage early marriage and give priority to settling down to stable family life. The pressure is more likely to be felt by women than men, and increases as individuals grow older.

Although marriage is likely to be prescribed at some stage of life as a remedy for all kinds of life problems, the images people have of marriage will be different. In various ways these images will be 'packaged' and 'sold' to the upcoming generation. Those who have experienced marriage may attempt to encourage curiosity and thoughtfulness through education of one kind or another. Those who regard marriage as a religious sacrament may be concerned to convey the seriousness of the undertaking through symbolism and ritual. There will also be the influence of soap operas, from *Neighbours* to *EastEnders*, which will portray marriage with a blend of romanticism and earthiness.

But none of these factors is likely to be as potent an influence upon future relationships as the early family experiences absorbed by the young child. In the primary attachment to the mother, infants experience some of the most intense physical and emotional experiences of life – the satisfaction of a full belly, the warmth of bodily closeness, the security based on being able to trust other people, the survival of hatred and release from fear. These and other experiences are repeated and reworked, first with other members of the family, and later with an extending circle of contacts outside the home. Along with hereditary endowments these experiences will go far to determine the kinds of adult they will grow into, the kinds of images they will form of themselves and those around them, and the kinds of relationships they will have with others. These are the experiences which, in a fundamental sense, are the most potent programme of education for marriage and family life and which form the blueprints for the next generation.

3. *Choices*

In Britain today the majority of people have more options open to them than their forebears had. Although we must not forget the sizeable minority who are caught in a poverty trap, during recent years wages and salaries have risen overall more than the cost of living, and educational opportunities have widened. Most people have considerable leeway as to how they spend their money over and above basic subsistence requirements. What were once considered luxuries may well, as standards of living have risen, now seem like necessities. We can choose to have more of this, less of that, travel here, there and further afield. With growing educational opportunities, choice of job or profession has widened, although industrial recession and demographic factors have limited the opportunities in some businesses and trades.

We also have more freedom as to how we behave within our ascribed or achieved class. Although there are regional differences, social and marital roles have become less clearly defined and structured than they were half a century ago. Cohabitation as a prelude to marriage is now an acceptable option. Greater availability of effective contraception has enabled partners to decide when to start a family and what size it will be. The limitation that can now be placed on the child-bearing and child-rearing years gives women a greater choice as to whether to return to work sooner, later or not at all. Easier divorce makes ending an unsatisfactory marriage a real possibility.

Changes in attitudes to authority, including parental and conjugal authority, have extended the choices open to women and young people. Husbands and fathers no longer have total legal authority over their wives and children. In what has been called 'The Age of Psychology', the development of the individual and his self-fulfilment has been promoted and stressed over and above obligations and duties to marriage partners, children and other relatives. The 'Age of Psychology' has also become the 'Age of the Charter of Individual Human Rights'.

THE BURDEN OF CHOICE

Such wealth of opportunity does not necessarily make life any easier. In some ways it can make it harder. It can be more comfortable to say, 'I had to do it', than 'I did not know what to do and then I decided . . .' Some of the decisions now open to us require a careful sifting of information and balancing of the pros and cons. The scales can be fairly evenly balanced. Sometimes the required information may be difficult to obtain and the implications of different courses of action hard to predict. Some people find the options bewildering and feel that, with many old values discarded, they have no solid core of new ones to take their places and guide them in their choice.

It often happens that the greater the area of choice, the less clear cut are the guidelines. We now live in what has been called a 'turbulent environment',[1] which is characterized by increased levels of complexity, interdependence and uncertainty. What happens in another country can within seconds affect life in our own country. Turbulence arises in a society because of an accelerating but uneven rate of change, and because of unpredictable connections between the increasingly interdependent parts.

With modern methods of communication throughout the world, our perceptions are constantly being enlarged and our attitudes and values are shifting. However, it is often difficult to distinguish between fact and fiction. What one hears said by others does not always match up with our own experience, and we can no longer look round expecting to find clear-cut models of behaviour. As we mentioned in the first chapter of this book, egalitarian marriage is now widely promoted as an ideal, but recent research indicates that there is a wide gulf between what is said to be happening in terms of sharing in marriage and what actually happens.

In a turbulent environment, diversity, contradiction and disjunction are the norm. We have to live with uncertainty and we have to be far more adaptable than previous generations. Modern life often tests the limits of human adaptation.

One of the contradictions is that although at some levels we have an immense range of choices, at other levels we are very much constrained by economic and social facts and pressures. Our society is still governed mainly by the demands of industry and commerce on men and the needs and demands of children on women. Husbands are usually higher earners than their wives and their jobs or careers take precedence over those of women.

Many women still marry for economic reasons, able to live better on their husband's earnings than on their own. Rented accommodation has become scarce; heavy mortgages often require two salaries for some years and can delay the date of marriage or cohabitation, or the start of parenting. Whereas more women than before can choose whether to work or not after the child-bearing years, raised expectations of living standards may make this feel less like a choice and more of a basic requirement. (Families living in poverty or relative poverty are today frequently characterized by having only one earner.) And once a choice has been made, this, in itself, imposes constraints.

Although there is much social and occupational mobility, and our choice of marriage partner is wider than it used to be, we are obviously most likely to meet and continue acquaintance with people used to similar standards of living, values and expectations. On the whole, at a social level, like marries like. When young people form a strong attachment to someone of another race or religion, parents and elders may well express surprise. They may not feel open to accepting that person into the family, very aware of having to make a conscious effort to put aside prejudices and stereotypes in order to get to know, like and accept him or her. They take the stranger to their heart less easily than the familiar friend. Reflecting the degree of adaptation required, parents may well express concern as to whether the match is viable.

While it is important to recognize the social constraints within which we exercise our choices, the more options there are available, the more psychological factors come into play. Our choices are partly governed by conscious processes of the mind – a rational weighing up of possibilities, advantages, disadvantages, wishes and motives – but also by unconscious factors of which, by definition, we are unaware. As we described in the last chapter, blueprints (some of which are not available to conscious recall) weigh heavily among the factors which determine our motives, choices and behaviour. Where loving and intimate relationships are concerned, we seem to be more strongly influenced by familial blueprints and unconscious preoccupations than by other factors. The more these blueprints exercise their influence, the less choice there seems to be and the more a particular course of action feels inevitable – a common experience for many people in their choice of partner. In short, choice is narrowed by internal as well as external constraints. When we speak of strong attachment or attraction between two people we are in the realms of love, the basis on which many people in our culture choose or are drawn towards their marriage partner. We are also in the realms of unconscious choice.

CHOICE OF LOVED ONE

It has been argued that romantic love is a relatively modern phenomenon, reserved in earlier times for the delight of troubadours and the illicit pleasures of the rich. Yet it has cast its spell since time immemorial – once the business of wizards and sorcerers, still the business of astrologers; once subject to aphrodisiacs, philtres and charms, now subject to immense commercialism. Classical literature tells us that through the centuries love was deemed to be compatible with a good marriage and in the Middle Ages canon law, by basing the validity of marriage on free consent, upheld love as a precursor of the union.

The verb to love is difficult to define as it covers such a range of emotion. The Oxford dictionary is cautious in its definition: 'to hold dear'; 'to be fond of'; 'to delight in'. It gets stronger when it includes 'to be addicted to'. When we talk of the in-love state, we are usually including strong sexual passion and an intensity of emotion not experienced in other affectionate and loving relationships. Loss of the loved one can raise the same intensity of emotion: a sense of betrayal, hatred of the betrayer, extreme jealousy of a rival – feelings over which a person may believe they have little or no control. Love and anger, it seems, are two sides of the same coin. The stronger the love, the stronger the rage when that love is not reciprocated. The opposite of loving is indifference, with its lack of feeling one way or the other. It is the strength of feeling associated with the in-love state that makes choice feel irrelevant.

Clearly we do not have full control over feelings. We either have them or we do not, although we can at times make a conscious effort to put certain feelings out of our minds. Some feelings are more easily dismissed than others, and some are more easily summoned up. Some can be so strong that regardless of the consequences they compel action. With other feelings we may be burdened by their strength, yet still be free enough to choose whether we express them to others by word or action, indulge them or keep a tight rein on them. There is immense variation between people in their ability to handle their feelings, and in the capacity of one person to handle different types of feeling. Strange as it may seem, some people have more difficulty in handling or expressing warm, loving feelings than negative, angry ones; or it may feel as if they have to keep a tighter reign on the loving feelings, which they perceive as making them more vulnerable to rejection and disappointment.

All of this suggests that while love is centred on feelings for another person, feelings for the self are never absent. Milton Erickson, a marital therapist, when asked how he would describe a good marriage, answered:

> . . . there are essentially four kinds of love. The infantile type of love, 'I love me.' The next state, 'I love the me in you. I love you because you are my brother, my mother, my father, my sister, my dog. The *me* in you.' Then the adolescent love, 'I love you because your dancing pleases me, and because your brains please me.' And the adult stage of love wherein, 'I want to love you and cherish you because I can find my happiness in your happiness. The happier you are the happier I will be. I'll find my happiness in yours . . .' So, the mature love is the capacity to find enjoyment in the enjoyment of the other person's enjoyment. *It works both ways.*[2] (Our italics)

Love can grow up, but is rarely totally altruistic. The best of lovings are mutual, with a fairly even amount of give and take, as much received as given. Erickson goes on to say that in good marriages all four types of love exist: I love me; I love me in you; I love your good qualities; and I enjoy the fact that you are happy. However, there needs to be a sizeable amount of the latter for the marriage to work. We shall be coming back in this chapter and the next to the problems that occur when choice is based on too much of 'I love me' and 'I love the me in you', but first we need to look at the basic capacity to realize some love for another, with its mix of self-regard and altruism.

Although everyone has the innate capacity to love and to enjoy another's happiness as well as their own, and to get themselves loved and their happiness enjoyed by others, not everyone can risk the experience in adult life. The realization of the capacity depends on the earliest blueprints and the infant's experiences of mutuality, giving and receiving or, sadly, its absence. The ability to love ourselves and another is formed in early childhood. As has been said, 'We love in as much as love was present in the first great affair of our lives!'[3]

In Chapter 2 we described the part played by our earliest love affairs in forming personal blueprints for living. We now return to the processes by which they are formed and consider their impact on freedom of choice.

THE FOUNDATIONS

According to Klein, a child psychoanalyst, babies are consumed with a primitive and innate rage when their needs are not met and they are in bodily discomfort.[4] The average, 'good enough' mother (to use the terminology of another analyst, Donald Winnicott) cleans, feeds, holds firmly and comforts the raging baby. Time and time again babies learn that their rage and hatred do not destroy the source of nourishment and love which is prepared to succour and relieve distress. Repeated experiences of regained enjoyment slowly mitigate the primitive fury.

At first infants cannot distinguish between themselves and others. Life is totally bad – a terrible 'Ow' – or totally good – a beautiful 'Mm' – and when distress is relieved it may well be as if they themselves have conjured up the goodness. In their omnipotence, they can delight in 'I love me.' Gradually they learn to discriminate, although for some time they cannot determine what is influencing the mother's movements towards or away from them. Later they acquire some idea of her motives and of their own. Once that is so, says Bowlby, 'the groundwork is laid to develop a much more complex relationship with each other, one that I term a partnership'. In the formation of the partnership and in the baby's increasing awareness of difference, the mother imparts more than nourishment and cleanliness; she lays the foundation of a future ability to trust and hope, to enjoy with another and to be grateful to another for that enjoyment. Love for another is one of the main derivatives of this awareness of difference (two bodies in different skins) and the accompanying gratitude when good things are provided: 'I love you because you are my mother and give me the good things I need.' From gratitude comes the desire to please: 'I want you to be happy too.'

People who have this early experience of their anger being mitigated by another and have learnt that their initial angry protest does, in fact, bring relief and comfort, learn two more important lessons. First, that anger is not necessarily destructive. It does not have to destroy love, but can be contained within it. Love is bigger. With this knowledge inside them, people do not have to be afraid of their own anger, nor their own assertiveness. They can allow themselves to feel them without undue anxiety. Through trial and error they learn how and where it is appropriate to express such feelings and when they will be effective. So they acquire some freedom of choice as to the how, when and where of using the anger of which they have command.

Second, related to the first and to the awareness of being in their own skin, they learn that it is proper and effective to signal for what they need. At first, their signals are just cries of protest. If these cries are heard and met, and therefore effective, the cry can, when the ability is acquired, be transferred into words: 'I want'; 'I am hungry'; 'I am hurt.' When words bring the required response there is less need to scream and it becomes all right to ask. And it becomes all right to ask even though the answer is sometimes 'No'. One 'No' does not mean eternal 'Noes'.

The child who does not learn to ask is seriously impaired in later life. This can result from either of two extremes of handling. On the one hand, there is the infant whose every need continues to be met before it is expressed (one whose mother cannot bear the weakest cry – perhaps she herself was left to cry for too long). This child fails to learn to be in touch with feelings and to form requests.

On the other hand, people whose words are not answered may have to spend a lifetime screaming for what they want or need, convinced that only if they demand loudly, cajole, beg, bully or threaten, will they obtain what they want. Or, with a continuing conviction that others will never meet their needs, they may have to get what they want by stealth or theft; they learn that only self can look after self. Again, if the early screams of protest have been severely punished, regard for their own need may feel too dangerous. The infantile, unmet scream may be repressed, either successfully or partially, at times breaking out from a normally controlled and reasonable adult. Those who have learnt that a scream never pays may lose all hope; even protest is useless.

If the ability to ask, to trust another to respond and to feel gratitude are three of the main derivatives of an early partnership and the basis of love, envy is one of the strongest antidotes to loving. It, too, has its roots in the innate, primitive anger and anxiety of infancy, when food and comfort were withheld. When the baby's need becomes ravenous, it feels insatiable. As infants slowly become aware of the mother as a separate person, they see her as the owner of a much needed resource. If she withholds beyond their as yet limited capacity for tolerance, their continuing rage seeks only to destroy what is in her. What she can provide is no longer experienced as goodness and, therefore, evokes no gratitude.

Unmitigated infantile anger, and subsequent envy of what the other possesses, has a murderous quality. In later childhood, these emotions may well be repressed, as parents and then teachers attempt, by a variety of means, to socialize young people. Such people may remain frightened, consciously or unconsciously, of the strength of their anger and possible loss of control. It has often been said that the non-neurotic person is one whose repressive mechanisms work well. When they do not work effectively, the unmitigated anger may well seep out in constant irritation over relatively trivial things or, as it seems to other people, may suddenly and unexpectedly break out with a degree of force inappropriate to the circumstances.

Foundations are laid in early months and years and subsequently built on. Or they can be shaken, the new and perhaps frail ability to trust, hope and feel gratitude needing to be re-established. Most toddlers experience a severe shaking of the foundations when the next child is born and they cease to be the baby. Are they totally replaced? Does another always come first? Or are they still loved, even though more grown up? They have to start to learn to share the love.

Sometimes foundations are shaken to the core by the premature death or prolonged absence of the main attachment figure. Such a shaking is experienced as supreme betrayal – total abandonment of the source of life and comfort. Because the theme of betrayal figures so often in fable, myth and legend throughout all cultures, it seems that it is something we must all know about at one level or another and need to have formalized in story form. It is important to remember that the word trust is meaningless if there is no possibility of betrayal, just as there can be no betrayal if there is no element of trust. We are not betrayed by enemy or foe, but by our nearest and dearest, or, at least, by our normally reliable friend.

We can guess that, despite a natural growth process, we all experienced a series of early betrayals as our mother expected and encouraged us to grow up and slowly emphasized her separateness and difference. Such betrayals, when not over-taxing the as yet limited mental resources of the infant, are compensated for by the acquisition of new much praised skills and satisfactions. (And failure to encourage infants to grow up and experience their own separateness and uniqueness is as much a betrayal of the concept of self as is the abandonment of support and pleasure in their developing maturity.) Yet betrayal of the initial oneness – the harmonious whole, a glorious, bodily, yet undefined goodness in which there is no distinction between the me and the you – is part of human experience, as is its loss. The search for love and the in-love state can be seen as an attempt to recreate the harmonious whole. This statement has been echoed through the ages – by Plato: 'Love is the desire and pursuit of the whole'; by Coleridge: 'Love is a desire of the whole being to be united to some thing, some being, felt necessary for its completeness'; and by the man in the street; 'My other half', or even 'My better half'; or in Erickson's terms: 'the "me in you"'.

THE 'ME IN YOU'

In biological terms, heterosexual love makes whole. Man cannot experience the fullness of his masculinity and powers of reproduction without a woman, and vice versa. In addition, both men and women have masculine and feminine genes within them, but their gender is normally recognized by one set of genes having predominance over the other. There is much argument as to how far different sexual traits are innate or socially conditioned. It is likely that social formulations have, over the ages, reflected innate differences. Some men and women who are sure of and comfortable with their predominant gender are able to express their 'other half', some people much less so. Close association with a member of the other sex, as in marriage, allows a wider range of response and action than either partner could have on their own. The husband keeps himself in touch with his feminity as expressed by his wife; she keeps herself in touch with her masculinity as expressed by her husband.

But the question remains, why do we fall in love with one person rather than another when many potential partners are available? Why is it that a specific person has the indefinable 'It' and another has not? What is the nature of this magnetic attraction?

We have two levels of answer to these questions. First, one of the main characteristics of attachment behaviour, which we outlined in the previous chapter and which derives from the study of animals and humans, is the specificity of the required caring figure. When safety is threatened, another figure will not do; ewe and lamb seek out their own. When overt attachment behaviour is at its peak in young children, it is the main attachment figure (usually the mother) who is needed.

Second, the specificity of who it is *safe* to love is related to the 'me in you': 'I love someone who reflects part of myself, sometimes a hidden or unacknowledged part of myself; I feel good with a you who either shares my feelings, expresses them for me or helps me to defend myself against them.' Most strong attachments are, we believe, based on a mixture of these three processes – identification of feeling, complementarity of feeling and mutual defensive avoidance of other feelings. All these three processes can be conscious or unconscious. The mix, the range and the flexibility of them relate back to early familial blueprints of how feelings were expressed, handled or avoided. We suggest that the more a person is in love and the less they are able to define what it is in the other that they love, the less free is the conscious choice and the more it relates to the 'me in you' and the search for psychological wholeness through another. Let us look at the three processes in more detail – the hopes and the fears invested in the processes and the inherent problems if one process is too predominant over the others.

IDENTIFICATION   Some people who have been rudely awakened to awareness of difference, who have never learnt to value the otherness of the other or feel safe with it, may need to search for love only with their mirror image. Likeness is safer than difference, and difference is to be feared. A marriage based mainly on likeness can be in trouble when too easy an assumption is made that the other must feel the same and when inevitable differences emerge and cannot be tolerated. Emergence of difference is often experienced as a shock to the whole system, a sudden puncturing of the illusion of sameness.

In the extremest form of love of the mirror image, a person does not form a close heterosexual attachment at all, remaining more comfortable and much safer in the love of a member of the same sex. (Many different early blueprints may play into this and compound the fear of the opposite sex, but we are not elaborating on this, as homosexuality is not the subject of this book.) Less extreme, but also narcissistic in their need for reflection of the self, some people manage to find a member of the opposite sex who, despite difference of gender, is in physical terms remarkably, even strangely, like them. This can be most apparent when beauty marries beauty. Beauty is often the object of envy by a plain person, yet people whose prettiness as children captivated the adults around them may grow up with a severe disadvantage. They often over-rely on their appearance as a means of relating, although they feel cheated when they perceive others as responding only to their physical attributes. Beautiful people are often surprisingly insecure, more so than those who fear they are not pretty or handsome enough to attract the opposite sex.

Identical twins growing up with their own image constantly near them, sometimes very in tune with what the other is thinking and feeling, may have a problem in their search for a marriage partner on several counts. First, it may be difficult for them to relinquish the closeness and identification with their twin in favour of a marriage partner. Second, they may seek this type of identification with a partner and be disappointed when they cannot find it. And third, their likeness to their twin can confuse possible suitors: which one does he want?

COMPLEMENTARITY Love of the other as a complement to the self is often quite conscious, with opposing social skills and personality traits openly admired. The calmness, even dullness, of one partner may be containing and useful to an excitable other, just as the more emotive response of the latter may engage and bring spontaneity into an otherwise stable and ordered life.

However, in the search for wholeness one partner may choose and use the other to express a feared or unrecognized part of the self, and this, by definition, is unconscious: 'I love the unrecognized me in you'. For example, Clive and Rose Greenacre's early blueprints had left them both distrusting dependency and the reliability of others, but they handled this problem in complementary ways. Rose was excessively clinging in her behaviour and anxious when Clive was either late, as he often was, or away on an extended business trip. She was slightly agoraphobic and did not go far from home on her own. Clive expressed his distrust and fear of being let down by a very detached attitude in all his relationships. He preferred to keep acquaintances as such, rarely divulged his feelings and placed little reliance on others. He could be quite casual in his attitude to his wife's anxiety and more often than not failed to let her know when he was delayed. However, on his belated homecomings, he indirectly reassured her that the needed person did return in the end. And he, so apparently casual – punitively casual – often irritated by her anxiety, could also rely on her being there for him, but without having to know about his own need for her to be safely where he had left her.

Ronald and Daphne Parker had a mutual problem in handling and using anger. Ronald's internal volcano was heavily repressed, Daphne's regularly exploding. He always had to be the one who calmed her down. However, her expression of anger kept him in touch with that unrecognized part of himself, just as his control gave her a much needed boundary. His success in calming her down reassured them both that anger could be tamed.

Greed for love, attention and praise was a problematic area for Bob and Joan Halton. Joan grew up feeling that she was loved less than her prettier younger sister. She found she could get the attention and praise she wanted only by achieving, being good and caring for that pretty little monster she so resented. To ask for more for herself and put herself in a position of coming first felt too greedy and dangerous. Bob, an only child, had no problem in expressing his greed. His mother had encouraged it, over-indulged him and assured him that he always came first. But he was fearful of greedy women. His mother had given him contrary messages. Despite her indulgence of him, she had kept him very much tied to her apron strings and had had great difficulty in relinquishing him to a wife. Several previous courtships had foundered on her disapproval.

We want to stress not only how marriage partners choose the complementarity of the other in handling difficult areas of feeling, but also how sensible this can be. We go so far as to say that in choice of partner it is a wise unconscious that falls in love with and marries its own unrecognized problem and then in marriage recreates the problematic situation. At least it keeps a person in touch with the problem. At best, it provides a chance of doing something about it – repairing a bit of the past, perhaps finding a new way of handling difficult feelings and making them less dangerous. When less dangerous, they can be owned and a person becomes a little more whole.

DEFENCES   Clive Greenacre, in his distrust, used his wife's agoraphobia as a defence against his own need to be sure of her being safely where he left her. Ronald Parker defended against his own expression of anger, but relied on his wife to be the exploder. Joan Halton used her husband to express the emotional greed of which she was so frightened in herself. In fact we can say that we never need to have our own feelings if we can be sure that our nearest and dearest will express them for us. And we never need our own defence if we can be sure that another will provide one for us.

There are various definitions of the phrase 'psychological defence'. We use the words in the sense of a psychic process by which the mind protects itself from undue or unbearable pain, anxiety or conflict. Psychologists often refer to a list of generally used defences: repression, denial, displacement, splitting, projection and reaction formation are the most commonly used. However, as we have already indicated, we believe that means of protection from psychic pain is not limited to this list; any feeling can be used to defend the self from any other feeling which is feared. For example, Ronald and Daphne could be using Daphne's expression of anger not only to protect Ronald from knowing about his own anger, but also to protect them both from underlying depressed feelings of which they are even more afraid. Anger can be used as a defence against depression, just as depression, sometimes defined as anger which has been turned inwards, can protect from overt anger or fear of violence. As we intimated previously in the section on identification, an over-emphasis on likeness can defend against the reality and fear of difference.

It is important not to despise the use of defences. We all use them much of the time and could not do without them. Our minds could not stand the constant battering of immediate reaction to the myriad perceptions to which we are subject all the time. For example, for much of the day we need to be able to repress or split off some feelings to enable us to concentrate or to use our intellects. The difference between mental health and mental ill-health is not in whether or not defences are used but in the flexibility or rigidity with which they are employed and in the mix between them, as opposed to the over-use of one defence rather than others.

One defence much used in the 'I love me in you' aspect of marriage is that of projection. Projection is the unconscious attribution to others of feelings that belong to the self. It is most often used when there is an internal conflict of feeling. If this conflict is too problematic, one feeling remains conscious and the opposing one is repressed but projected into another person who expresses it. When it is expressed by the marriage partner the internal conflict is externalized, sometimes on a daily basis. If this happens in moderation and can be relinquished, little harm is done. For example, Joan Halton may use Bob to express the greed of which she is afraid, then protest about the greed he displays. If her protest is effective, she becomes less frightened of her own greed and more able to own and express it for herself. They may then have more flexibility as to who is allowed to be the greedy one. The underlying quarrel in marriage is frequently about how often each can be allowed to be the baby.

However, continued and inflexible projection can intensify fear of the problematic feeling. Joan's unconscious encouragement of Bob's selfishness may lead him to more extreme behaviour (in psychoanalytic terms, her projection leaves him carrying a 'double dose'). This may confirm Joan's fear of greed and make it more frightening for her to know about her own. The more one partner complains about the behaviour of the other but remains firmly attached to that person, the more we can suspect that a massive projective system is in operation. When we would expect a feeling to be expressed to some extent by both partners but instead one person is quite overcome with emotion while the other is apparently untouched, we may assume that one carries and expresses the feeling for both.

We mentioned earlier in this chapter that an unreal identification with the partner can be used as a defence against fear of difference. So can an over-emphasis on difference be used defensively against fear of excessive closeness. People who have felt too impinged upon in childhood, too taken over, not allowed to experience their own feelings, may bolster their fragile sense of identity by marrying someone ostensibly very different, but with a similar underlying fear of being swamped. Although 'mixed' marriages between people of different races or cultures are made for a variety of reasons, conscious and unconscious, some are necessitated by the need to have constant reassurance of difference: for example, a skin of another colour. Marrying out of one's own culture is a rejection of that culture and some thing or things feared within it. Some people, for example, feel less constrained in a language other than their mother tongue when they have felt too burdened by words and idioms used by their mother. In freeing themselves from this burden they may need to make their escape into another language or culture, even by establishing geographical distance over thousands of miles of ocean.

Others, terrified of intimacy and closeness, use quarrels as a means of maintaining distance. In marital therapy it is often noticeable that although a couple are asking for help to sort out their problem, so that they may have the closeness and intimacy for which they yearn, fear overcomes hope, and whenever things start to improve one of them can be relied upon to start up the next quarrel.

There are people whose early experience of bodily closeness, intimacy and care has been so uncomfortable or so traumatic that they dare not risk a repetition of such pain. If, despite this, social and economic pressures lead them to marry, they may find a partner who also needs to avoid close involvement, emotional or physical. They may even marry quite young to escape the pressures of the courting scene, but in these cases choice of partner is based more on the need for a mutual defence against a mutual problem than in hope of a mutual problem being resolved. In these terms, the marriage, rather than some aspects of it, is defensive. Some people very frightened of their homosexual leanings may consciously or unconsciously enter a defensive marriage to protect themselves from these feelings. What better proof of heterosexuality than to be married?

We could say we can divide the world into two, although with many shadings in between: those who marry to avoid their problems and those who marry to tangle with them. The former, not having fallen in love, or with few of their emotions engaged, often continue to feel cheated. The latter, whose emotions are firmly engaged are, we believe, the majority.

For this majority, the unconscious choice of partner is governed by a mix of hopes and fears, the prospect of repairing and making whole and the fear of doing so. Most married couples will tangle with some mutual residual problems and leave others firmly alone, retaining some well-defended areas in their personalities and in their partnership.

In the first few years of marriage, before the decision to have a baby is made, reparative work is about intimate pairing and what was felt to have been betrayed in the first partnership of life with the main attachment figure. When the intimate twosome is established, some early experiences repaired, some old ghosts laid to rest, a couple are ready to make what then can be a choice – to create a baby or not.

THE OPTION OF PARENTING

With reproduction essential for the maintenance of the species, we can but assume that there is a basic biological drive to create. This can be expressed by people saying that they feel they want a child for their fulfilment as human beings. Others may talk about a deep urge. Some never query that sooner or later they will have a child or several children. Others know about the pleasure they get from children. Having enjoyed their own childhood and experienced their parents' delight in them, they want to repeat the good experience from the position of parent, and have few fears about this. It is as if from their own experience of good parenting they know inside themselves what parenting is about.

Some women in early adulthood may feel very unmaternal and not at all sure whether they wish to burden themselves with what they see as the cares and stresses of parenthood. They may delay the decision, in confusion or conflict over the choice now open to them; but their bodies may give them messages. They become more aware of other people's babies, wanting to hold and touch them. 'I've started to feel broody,' they may be heard to say. Sometimes the internal conflict of wanting/not wanting a baby, wanting/ fearing having one, is expressed in menstrual pain or premenstrual tension. Have I conceived or not? Am I relieved or disappointed by the menstrual flow?

Social encouragement for starting a family is strong. When peers are becoming absorbed by the new life-style that a baby brings, a couple may feel left behind if they do not embark on this too. Would-be grandparents can express their disappointment at not acquiring the longed-for grandchild. Such is the general expectation that married couples will have children that those who do not want them, or want to put parenthood off a few more years, or sadly learn that they cannot conceive, find themselves having to respond to veiled or not so veiled queries. They can feel criticized, even stigmatized, and in need of group support. It is ironic, as research into the feelings and behaviour of childless couples has shown, that the voluntarily childless often shield themselves from criticism by implying a fertility problem, whereas the involuntarily childless find it difficult to admit their infertility and leave others believing they have chosen to forgo the experience of parenthood.

Babies are conceived for a variety of reasons apart from basic urges – some not so laudable: to save a marriage which is going wrong; to keep control over a wayward partner who shows signs of straying from the fold; in competition with a sister who has recently conceived or in determination to produce the first grandchild. As we have stated before in this chapter, the greater the choice that is open to people, the more psychological factors, often unconscious, come into play.

When a child is born and a twosome becomes a threesome, more blueprint patterns begin to operate, as they do again when second and subsequent children are born. The art of managing a threesome is for one of the three to allow the other two to pair, sure in the knowledge that other pairings can easily be restored and the individuals flexibly interchange with each other. For some people this is very difficult, especially when they have no internal model from their early experience of family life to assist them. But as in the choice of a partner, so in the choice of parenthood, people may attempt to repair and correct early experiences of threesomes and foursomes. In giving to their children what they felt they needed and did not have themselves, they obtain gratification and solace.

It is noticeable that parents often react against their own experience so that, for example, if they were brought up in a too restrictive atmosphere with little spoiling, they may spoil and leave their children without enough boundaries and routine. In spoiling the children they are vicariously spoiling themselves. People who have felt severely betrayed by the birth of a younger sibling may find they have more difficulty in handling a second child than the first, but this does not deter them from bearing that second child. The problematic area needs to be repeated. It is obviously difficult for a parent to help a child through a developmental hurdle which he has not properly encompassed himself, but parents and children can grow up together, or, as we might say, children can bring up their parents.

When considering the options now open to us in respect of parenting, it is important to understand the enormity of some of the choices that can be made today. As well as the selection of family size, there are choices to allow or to refuse life to a healthy or damaged foetus, to agree to artificial insemination by husband or other donor, and to opt for *in vitro* fertilization. Not only do these decisions carry immense implications for the future of parents and children, but they are open to criticism from relatives, friends, public opinion and pressure groups upholding opposite views. In addition, these options widen the arena for disagreement between partners. How is a basic disagreement of this nature resolved? Who gives in and with what misgivings? When things go wrong, who feels blamed or guilty about having persuaded? Never has the burden of choice been so heavy. So much knowledge and maturity is required to make this type of choice from a properly informed base.

OYSTERS

In this chapter we have concentrated on two major life choices, the choice of marriage partner and, more briefly, whether to parent or not. By illustrating how unconscious factors influence these choices we have raised the question of how much choice we actually exercise. Is the world our oyster, or is it not?

We are not arguing that everything is predetermined. Yes, early blueprints are influential. We cannot escape our past, nor deny our feelings, which are so often less rational than our intellects. But we can follow or reject the blueprints; we can consciously master some, but not all; and, as we have emphasized, unless all hope is killed off by dire early environments, a psychological growth process continues throughout life. In seeking to promote the realization and wholeness of human nature, we attempt to correct our early unsatisfactory experiences. In doing so we often heal old psychological wounds. In order to resolve our underlying conflicts and problems, we find partners who enable us to replay old scenes. When we fall in love the wisdom of the unconscious takes the lead.

As a marriage continues, and the family moves through its different stages, many other major choices will have to be made, including the most difficult one of whether or not to end a marriage. We shall come back to these in later chapters. Here it is important to note that, despite the burden of many of the choices we can now make, people leave themselves with just as weighty a problem by refusing to recognize the options open to them, either putting themselves too easily in other people's hands or not allowing themselves enough space to make an informed choice. For example, in the infertility clinics, the patient's yearning for a child meets the drive, satisfaction and status inherent in or accorded to technical brilliance. Yearning and brilliance clasp hands and sweep along together. People desperate to conceive can sometimes enter fertility programmes without enough space to query how far they are prepared to go, to resolve any differences between the partners, or to mourn their personal loss in not being able to produce a child naturally.

Some people are unable to make choices because they feel they must have everything and cannot accept the loss that is inherent in exercising choice. For example, some women in a financial position to stop work and start a family are loath to give up their careers for a period, knowing they may lose out in the long term. Having realized their ambition to combine their career with child-rearing, they remain torn between and exhausted by the demands of job and baby, with ever-decreasing satisfactions in both spheres.

To whom or what are they primarily committed? In the next chapter we consider the subject and problems of commitment.

4. *Commitment*

CONTRACTS AND COVENANTS

The marriage ceremony involves a couple in a public contract – a legal commitment to each other and only to each other, bigamy being a punishable crime. The contract is witnessed by others and duly recorded. This legal bond can be severed only through a court of law, and even then the court may insist on one partner continuing to make provision for the other. Society lays down the basic rules of the marriage contract.

In addition, the couple make a public covenant to love and to cherish, to help and to comfort in both prosperity and adversity. Despite the number of marriages broken by divorce, it seems that most young people make their vows in good faith, intend to keep them and see themselves as committed to the other for life. That is not to say that they may not have doubts, be nervous of, or awed by, the large step they are taking. The feelings that are carried up the aisle or into the registry office are presumably countless.

The public covenant is underwritten by an emotional covenant, partly unconscious, and binding in its claims. The emotional covenant is often the first to be formed. It can hold couples together in a way that may seem to the outsider against all reason. And it can continue to press its claims beyond divorce and even the death of one partner.

The process of making a commitment to marriage usually involves a number of stages. Whether or not it is good fortune to fall in love with the person you marry, our culture dictates that this is the basis of proper marriage. The exclusive and private stage of falling in love is followed by one in which commitment is made public. A couple may begin living together or formally announce their engagement. Then follows the wedding ceremony, marking the beginning of marriage proper and the myriad negotiations of the early years of married life.

The experience of falling in love is frequently the first intimation for two people that they may end up married to each other. An emotional covenant begins to be formed. For many, the loved person has to be won. There are no guarantees that love will be reciprocated. Manoeuvres have to be carefully planned, subtly executed and brought to a successful conclusion. The old phrase, 'all is fair in love and war', suggests how low we may stoop in order to conquer. The chase and the conquest take so much time and energy that there is often little room for anything else in life. For some it is difficult to acknowledge love until they are sure they are loved in return. For some the love of the chase becomes an end in itself. There are those who spend their lives courting the unobtainable, pursuing impossible dreams; and there are the Don Juans and *femmes fatales* who prefer to travel rather than to arrive, leaving behind them a path strewn with broken hearts. For some, life becomes one long struggle to conquer; the commitment is to conquest.

When a conquest is made, the oneness of the individual is often superseded by a state of oneness in the partnership. In order to hold on to what is most important to them it is as if the courting couple enter into an unconscious agreement with each other not to expose differences, even if this results in negating themselves. Outward signs of selfless generosity override the expression of personal needs and insecurities, except when the relationship is threatened by the advances of a third party. Differences are played down and the self surrendered in what can become a metaphysical experience of the kind described by John Donne:

> *Our hands were firmly cimented*
> *With a false balme, which thence did spring,*
> *Our eye-beames twisted, and did thred*
> *Our eyes, upon one double string;*
> *. . . Our soules, (which to advance their state*
> *Were gone out,) hung 'twixt her, and mee.*

In this state it can seem as if there is a drive not to know too much about the other person. In *Middlemarch*, George Eliot records Dorothea's state of mind as she prepares to marry Mr Casaubon, a man she hardly knows:

She filled up all the blanks with unmanifested perfections, interpreting him as she interpreted the works of Providence and accounting for seeming discords by her own deafness to the higher harmonies. And there are many blanks left in the weeks of courtship which a loving faith fills with happy assurance.

The idealized state of being in love is an insecure condition. There is so much to be won and so much at stake. Living on cloud nine is intoxicating and precarious. There is a fear of being found wanting, even found out, and thus the constant threat of a plummeting descent from heaven. There is a dread of falling from grace. The process of engaging, seducing and conquering is a time of extreme emotions, of high hopes and despair, of jealousy and triumph, of intense agitation and prolonged inactivity. The intensity of life at this time led Congreve to compare courtship favourably with marriage as 'a very witty prologue to a rather dull play'.

The process of idealizing one's partner, turning a blind eye to faults or discrepancies between what is and what is desired, can perform a useful function. It spurs people into making a commitment to each other. With commitment and sufficient trust comes more freedom to get to know the other person as he or she really is. A diminishing fear of loss allows some separateness to develop in the partnership; a two-person relationship which is more substantially based on how things really are between the partners begins to emerge. As the move towards a shared life begins to take hold, the process of finding a mutually comfortable balance between being together and being apart begins in earnest. A more critical appraisal becomes possible as partners step back to regard each other. The realities of what living with this other person might be like begin to be registered and weighed up. Although a measure of ambivalence is quite usual, it is at this point that a decision is made about going public.

With the greater prevalence of cohabitation as a prelude to marriage, many couples feel they make their public commitment to each other when they set up house together and sign the joint mortgage form. They may think that they are realistically aware of what they are letting themselves in for and what they need to know about each other's strengths and weaknesses.

The period of cohabitation is often thought of as a trial marriage. It certainly is a trial – a trial in living together and forming a partnership. It is also a public statement about being together. But in terms of its being easier and cheaper to disband and its not carrying the same legal authority, it is not the same as marriage. It is a half-way house, an intermediate commitment with no binding promises for the future and a built-in escape route. The public ceremony, the ritual, the signing of the contract, which can speak so powerfully to the inner world of the subjects, is absent.

The time many cohabiting couples choose to legalize their union is when they are pleased enough with each other as partners to start a family. For them, making the legal contract of marriage may feel like a re-statement of a previous covenant and, therefore, not so emotionally decisive and fraught. They may feel less burdened by the weight of decision and freer to enjoy both ceremony and party.

They, and those who have not cohabited, may cross the threshold into marriage without much of a backward glance, feeling sure they have 'arrived', thankful for having arrived, found their mate, achieved their haven, caught up with their friends, pleased or escaped from their parents. For women without previous commitment to their own career, dependent as they still often are on the normally higher earnings of men, there may be the excitement of starting their life project, married to their husband's job and caring for him and their much hoped-for children.

Others may be more aware of what they are leaving behind in making their commitment. They have to come to terms with a loss of freedom, a loss of the chase. Some may have a thought, even a regret, for the ones that got away – those they might have married but now will not. Some, when reaching their wedding day, may find it difficult to smile, feeling unhappily trapped, persuaded either by lover or parents into a marriage for which they do not feel ready. Others, perhaps the most doubting, may not dare to let themselves know their qualms. Their anxiety may be displaced on to the actual ceremony, making the responses correctly, being the centre of attention, or on to details of the reception or party to be held afterwards.

The wedding ceremony publicly marks the beginning of commitment to another through marriage. Family and friends are drawn together to witness the covenant and contract the couple make, to launch them into their new life together, and to provide practical help in setting up home. This public celebration is still usually followed by the private honeymoon, despite the fact that for many it will not be the first holiday they have had together. The honeymoon is likely to be the more enjoyable for that, no longer burdened by the weight of expectation, and sometimes fear, that spoilt the experience for some in days gone by. But the question remains – why marry?

Such is the strength of social pressure that many such couples want their children to have married parents. Fathers who want to exercise shared responsibility for their children may still need the security of the married state; named putative fathers, although legally required to support their offspring, still have limited rights in respect of them. Although two thirds of the children born out of wedlock are registered by both parents, and illegitimacy is on the increase, we in Britain have not reached the position arrived at in Sweden where, since 1 January 1988, partners who live together outside marriage are afforded the same legal rights as those who are married.

THE NEED FOR CONTAINMENT

As well as these social reasons, the commitment of marriage provides a secure framework within which the personal negotiations about space, needs, differences and roles can continue. The legal bond can be a useful container while partners struggle to come to terms with the 'me in you', the phenomenon we described in the last chapter.

When the inner world needs the security of a legally endorsed status, marriage can provide it. But when the inner world is frightened of commitment for one reason or another, the external legal authority seems to accentuate that fear, raising feelings of being trapped. Some couples whose cohabitation has worked well for them may be surprised, hurt or bewildered when, legally married, they find their relationship deteriorating.

Such deterioration may not necessarily result from the proclamation of commitment. If the marriage has been timed to coincide with starting a family, the pregnancy, or the move from a pair to a threesome, may have · more bearing upon the problems that arise. But it is likely that within the safety of the legal bond partners shake off some aspects of their public persona and expose more of themselves, particularly those problematic areas of their personalities with which unconsciously they wish to engage.

Just as a young child needs to be contained, given a safe and secure haven from which to explore and develop mastery of skills and to which to retreat when his efforts fail, so too might an adult need security in order to develop fully. Within the legal container of marriage, the idealization and illusion so characteristic of the in-love state can take a nasty knock. The person behind the conquering persona is allowed to emerge as he or she really is. Not only is this inevitable in day-to-day living together, but also, we believe, it is a proper use of containment. In the drive to make whole or, at least, a bit more whole, partners may need to regress in order to go forward again. Containment allows for regression. Old unresolved conflicts may need to be exposed rather than hidden or disguised.

In the last chapter we described how Bob and Joan Halton had been drawn together – had 'chosen' each other – by an unconscious preoccupation with handling their emotional greed. In their courtship, Joan stressed her good sense and ability to care. Bob did not overplay his obvious selfishness. In John Donne's terms, they had acknowledged each other as 'one another's best', but 'saw not what did move'.

In Joan Halton's attempt to be more whole, she needed to know more about her desire to come first, at least for part of the time, rather than always maintaining the veneer of premature maturity she had felt forced into adopting as a child. But can she allow herself to get in touch with that needy infant inside her adult self, or does she always have to be the carer, the non-greedy adult, leaving Bob Halton to express all the emotional greed for them both? (What was need in a child can be seen and experienced as greed in an adult.) As Jung said, an attempt to leave behind the child which still lives in us all, denies a part of ourselves and results in behaviour of a very childish, as opposed to childlike, kind.

What happens when the unconscious child in Joan Halton finds yet again that she is always losing out, this time to her husband, to his old car on which he dotes or to his mother who is still demanding so much of his time and attention, and that he appears to be forgetting that he is now married and has new first loyalties? And does Bob Halton have to use his old car or the demands of his mother to protect him from yet another demanding woman, whom he senses beneath the caring, loving girl he married? Now safely married, does he need to overstate his determination to come first, constantly afraid that if he gives an inch, he will inevitably lose a mile?

Both of them want to be close and both need to repair their inner confusion about what they can allow themselves. But, as is common, they are also afraid of what they most want. Joan Halton is disturbed by an old guilt related to the underlying resentment and fury she felt in respect of her younger sister who always seemed to be allowed to come first. Bob Halton, not guilty enough, but confused by his mother's spoiling and manipulative efforts to keep him for herself, is petrified of being taken over completely. If they can overcome their fears, they have a chance of doing something about their mutual problem, now explicit between them.

So, the big question is, can they have the necessary row? Can Joan Halton, within the safety of marriage, dare to protest in a way that gets the protest heard in a way she was not able to do with her mother? Can Bob

Halton hear the protest and risk giving up some of his 'I love me'? Can she get a bit more of 'I love me', and feel loved and pleased? Can a row about the endless Saturday afternoons he now spends bent over the bonnet of his old car be used as a vehicle for their underlying struggle? Can he, after the row is made up and she has something for herself, be relinquished back to his car, knowing that she is not as greedy as he feared? Can the car be allowed to be just a car, no longer a symbol of defence against possible demands, feelings about a prettier younger sister or a manipulating mother?

For many couples, this type of row out of bed, often made up in bed, does some useful repairing. There are many issues people have to address in the aftermath of courtship which are in contrast to the wishes and hopes experienced during it. But young couples are often surprised, even shocked, by the ferocity of the rows that can suddenly blow up in the first year or two of marriage. This is not how they perceived each other in the courtship. The rows may be triggered by a seemingly trivial incident, but it is not felt as trivial when it symbolizes past conflicts and needs. Usually one constant theme related to the shared preoccupation of the couple underlies the seemingly different causes of rows and arguments. We shall develop and illustrate this point in the next chapter. Here we are talking of the emotional covenant, the often unconscious commitment to make the selves of the two partners more whole through the interchange between them – a commitment to stay with the struggle of maturation within the relationship.

As we stated in the first chapter of this book, the developmental task of marriage is to convert the unconscious choice of partner into a conscious commitment. To do this requires some ability to acknowledge and manage one's own infantile feelings rather than inflexibly to project them into the other. Many couples stick with this covenant and the hope invested in it, and they make something of the struggle it entails. Bob and Joan Halton did so. Joan learned to ask more for herself without feeling too guilty about it. Bob learned to demand a bit less without confirming his worst fears. They have solved something important for themselves in the turn and turn about of a twosome. They still have a problem in managing the demands of Bob's mother, but this is now a shared problem which they discuss and handle together rather than a seat of battle for the two women with Bob torn between them. They will, no doubt, have further struggles when they start a family and more figures are competing in the hierarchy of need. However, their ability to tangle with the issue in the first place, and their success in doing so, will give them confidence to face those struggles when they arise again.

Many other couples stay with the commitment to a shared problem but fail to resolve it. The hope and fear is kept in fairly equal balance. Hope keeps the partners together; fear militates against any resolution. Clive and Rose Greenacre, also described in the last chapter, continued to live out their shared problem of fearing abandonment. It was as if their covenant was both to keep the problem alive and yet to ensure they did nothing about it.

Between them they expressed the opposing feelings so often displayed by young children in the peak age of attachment: on the one hand, the protest and fury about being left – cries of rage – and then a sullen refusal to acknowledge and come to the mother; on the other hand, the desperate yearning for the loved one and a need to cling and not let go. The mind of a young child is not yet strong enough to hold the two conflicting emotions. As a result one set of feelings is expressed while the other is repressed. This is the defence of splitting. At the age when it first occurs in respect of strong contrary feelings, the young child needs his parents to understand that the greater the yearning, the greater the protest. Within their firm containment, he can slowly learn about holding mixed feelings – loving and hating the same person. If left too long in a situation of abandonment, the split is not healed and comes to be used as a predominant defence, as it did with Clive and Rose Greenacre.

Rose expressed only the infantile yearning and clinging. Any anger about Clive's absences and frequent lateness remained firmly repressed. In contrast, Clive repressed all his earlier yearnings for closeness, but continued to express the old protest in his detached manner to all and sundry, and in his constant irritation with his wife's agoraphobia and anxiety as to his whereabouts. Usually his anger seeped out in irritation; just occasionally his partial defence broke down and he erupted in an explosion of fury.

Despite the difficulties in their relationship they were unable to part. The fear of abandonment and being on their own was stronger than the discomfort of the existing situation. For them, separation symbolized the loss of hope. By staying together they were at least keeping their problem alive, even if failing to resolve it.

This common type of defensive splitting between married couples is often seen most clearly in retrospect when for some reason the joint defence is breached. In therapy, Rose Greenacre managed to get in touch with the anger she had previously been unable to feel consciously. Clive Greenacre, then expressing only his own anger and not hers as well, became less irritable. Rose, in her newly felt anger, started to complain about Clive's detached behaviour. As her anger was released, she became less agoraphobic.

She even thought that she might leave him. Clive then became less sure of her whereabouts and so of himself. She was no longer safely where he had left her and waiting for his return. She no longer provided him with a defence against his own yearning for safety which had been so well hidden behind his off-hand behaviour. Only then, when she was no longer expressing the yearning for him, did he learn of his own need. Faced with the threat of her desertion he was almost in a state of collapse, sometimes feeling quite suicidal. He, previously so detached, was now begging her not to leave him. These changes meant that they needed to form a new covenant based on some understanding of their mutual fears, their tendency to split their feelings between them, and their need to respect each other's yearnings and protests, now more readily experienced by each of them. They needed to understand that, at times, one or other symbolized the abandoning parent, reactivating in the other the child's need to protest or cling.

The underlying emotional covenant in some marriages is clearly expressed by one partner asking to be contained, the other being prepared to contain. Clive and Rose Greenacre's initial commitment could be seen in these terms, Rose in effect saying, 'Keep me safe, let me cling', Clive continuing to allow her to do so despite his irritation.

Jung wrote vividly about this type of covenant.[1] He suggested that the one who asks for containment usually has a simpler personality than the container who has a tendency to dissociate. He said, 'The one who is contained feels himself living entirely within the confines of his marriage; outside the marriage there exist no essential obligations and no binding interests.' The container, on the other hand, with his tendency to dissociate, 'has an especial need to unify himself in an undivided love', but finds the simpler personality of his partner does not complement and satisfy the diverse facets of his own.

According to Jung, a simpler nature works on a more complicated one 'like a room that is too small', not allowing the partner enough space. The more complex partner gives the simpler nature too much space, so that he does not know where he belongs. The more complicated feel they cannot be contained 'in such a small room' and then start 'spying through the window'. The more the contained attempts to cling, the more the container feels 'shut out of the relationship'. The greater the attempt to cling, the less the container can respond, thereby providing confirmation of the insecurity which feels so painful.

We have found that these roles are not always as clearly divided as may appear at first sight. The obvious and conscious container is sometimes unconsciously contained and vice-versa. For example, Rose Greenacre's agoraphobia was a useful container for Bob Greenacre.

The reader may remember Irene and Soames in *The Forsyte Saga*. Irene, with an apparently much more complicated nature, felt restricted and confined by the simpler-natured Soames:

> He was seldom indeed far from Irene's side at public functions, and, even when separated by the exigencies of social intercourse, could be seen following her about with his eyes, in which were strange expressions of watchfulness and longing . . .
>
> It was hard, when a man worked as hard as he did, making money for her – yes, and with an ache in his heart – that she should sit there, looking – as if she saw the walls of the room closing in.

Irene felt increasingly outside the marriage and started 'spying through the window' at the more complex-seeming Bosinney. The more Soames pushed, the more she felt alienated and the more he felt rejected, the vicious circle culminating in the so-called rape. Yet it was clear after Irene left him that she, too, was badly in need of a container, and finally found one in Young Jolyon.

Marriage partners are, perhaps, in the greatest difficulty when both are desperately seeking only to be contained, when neither can perceive the equivalent need in the other and provide accordingly. Then they become enmeshed in a desperate struggle about who is to be the baby. But we could say that in any marriage it is important for both partners to be able to contain and at times to say 'enough is enough'.

TRAPS

We mentioned earlier in this chapter that some people feel uncomfortable or trapped by the public contract of marriage, yet still allow themselves to be married. In some cases this may be a result of parental pressure and an earlier lack of encouragement to grów up and exercise adult autonomy. Marriage may feel yet one more place into which they have been pushed, one more area in which they have not been allowed to exercise their own choice. For others, the feeling of being trapped may arise from an early blueprint drawn up when they were literally helpless and unable to do anything about an intolerable situation or to get out of it on their own. The feeling of helplessness then continues to overshadow and influence later relationships. These people may need to get married – trapped – to prove that they can get out, that divorce is not impossible, to discover that they can influence and do something about the situation. Many otherwise inexplicable early divorces are about proving that one person can get out of a trap and another can let him or her go. Hopefully once will be enough, but not always. Some of the 'trapped' learn that a trap is not so bad after all; some traps can prove quite comfortable or can be modified to suit the individual.

There will be those who have gloried in the excitement of the chase and the passion of sex during courtship. Once married and committed to their partner, they may find excitement has flown out of the window. Some loss of excitement is inevitable. One of the many issues young people have to address in the aftermath of courtship is that they and their partners have feet of clay. Married life is partly about living with ordinariness. Most people want to be special and know they are special to their loved and chosen partner. But acceptance of ordinariness is also important. In Patrick White's *The Free Man*, Stan and Amy Parker are comforted only by habit '. . . like warm drinks and slippers', and in their emotionally empty house '. . . dusty light spilled from the windows. That was all.' Yet there is a place for drinks and slippers, and many younger and older couples can know about their mutual ordinariness so that they do not have to strive, posture or compete; and yet they still keep a specialness and excitement in each other alive.

In contrast, other people who are afraid of being ordinary and who miss the diversion of continual excitement may need to create a series of crises and emotionally charged situations to reassure themselves that they are alive. Such people often have a fragile sense of identity or are desperately frightened of a feeling of emptiness within themselves. As the protagonist in Kafka's *Conversation with a Suppliant* confessed: 'There has never been a time in which I have been convinced from within myself that I am alive.' Sometimes the crises are kept within the marriage. Sometimes, when much excitement was previously invested in the chase and conquest of courtship, the partners may need to continue to reassure themselves of being able to win love and move from one sexual conquest to another outside the marriage. Some partners, unsure of their loveability, may use affairs to get themselves reclaimed by their partner. The underlying covenant may be concerned with constant reclamation – reclaiming and being reclaimed.

Other couples, not afraid of ordinariness, may also find they are unable to create any of their own excitement within the commitment of marriage. They use ordinariness as a defence against excitement. In these cases their blueprint continues to give stern warnings that excitement in the home is dangerous. Too many early messages of 'Don't get excited, it'll only end in tears' have become etched in the mind. Often a fear of violence underlies the command of safety and prohibition against excitement. For some people excitement is only possible outside marriage. The commitment is to what is safe.

But why, we can ask, is excitement permissible outside marriage, and not within? What is the taboo on life and liveliness inside the family? The answer is often connected with incestuous fears. Once married, the partner can take on the shadow of a forbidding parent: 'Sex is dirty; sex is bad.' If the parent of the opposite sex was unconsciously seductive with this adult when a young child, and if the excitement of the love of and for this parent was felt to be too dangerous, or was disapproved of by the parent of the same sex, passion and excitement within marriage may continue to be forbidden by an inner imperative.

An American writer, Searles, wrote vividly about the importance of acknowledging strong, romantic feelings between parents and children of the opposite sex.[2] Speaking of his daughter, he said,

> I used at times to feel somewhat worried when she would play the supremely confident coquette with me and I would be enthralled by her charms, but then I came to the conviction, some time ago, that such moments of relatedness could only be nourishing for her developing personality as well as delightful to me. If a little girl cannot feel herself able to win the heart of her father, her own father who has known her so well and so long, and is tied to her by mutual blood-ties, I reasoned, then how can the young woman who comes later have any deep confidence in the power of her womanliness.
>
> And I have every impression, similarly, that the Oedipal desires of my son . . . have found a similarly lively and whole-hearted feeling response in my wife.

In continuing to speak of healthy relationships between children and parents, Searles emphasized the resolution of the Oedipal strivings, not just by the child's identification with the parent of the same sex, not just by the final taboo and containment of the feelings, but also by the parent's renunciation of the reciprocated romantic feelings with a real sense of loss, and also by the love between the parents to which the child owed his existence. Firm acknowledgement and containment of what are natural, but could be dangerous, feelings in childhood offer a useful blueprint to be carried into marriage. So, too, does the ability of parents to relinquish the young developing adult first to boyfriend or girlfriend, and finally to marriage partner.

CONFLICTING COMMITMENTS

People make many different commitments in the course of a lifetime. Some of these are compatible with the commitment made to a spouse, others compete for priority. Their nature changes over time and requires couples to renegotiate their covenant with each other time and time again.

From the outset, there may be conflict between the commitment of marriage and a commitment to parents. The continuing popularity of 'mother-in-law' jokes reinforces a universally recognized truth that marriage does not necessarily release people from the grip of their parents. That pull may have been stronger in the past than today. Nowadays there are opportunities for men and women to live away from home without getting married. Yet all couples have to make the break from home, emotionally if not physically, if they are to be free to make a marriage work. Even today, the expense and shortage of houses means that many couples will start married life living with one or other of their sets of parents. There is, therefore, a triangular situation to be resolved by all couples when establishing their marriage. Who is to come first? This question can become a major source of friction. One young wife described the problem in terms which will be recognizable to many young newly-weds:

'. . . we were both pulling in opposite directions, and I felt Brian was siding with his mother rather than standing up for me or remaining in the middle. He was not supporting me in the way I felt he should support me. We actually split up for a few days because his mother sent a Christmas card to him and not to me. I said, "Why can't you tell your mother now we're married she must send her Christmas card to both of us", but he couldn't tell her.'

Early in marriage a re-ordering of priorities is necessary, and some couples can run into trouble if their commitment to, or dependence upon, healthy robust parents cannot be allowed to take second place to their commitment to their new partner. But it is unwise to assume that parents will inevitably pose a problem when they are placed first. Some marriages are based on a tacit, if not explicit, agreement that parents have prior claims. Some people marry into families rather than commit themselves to a partner. Later in marriage a particularly keen sense of commitment may be felt towards aged or ailing parents. Obviously there is less conflict if the commitment is shared by both partners, but it can become a source of tension and disagreement.

Parents are not the only people to be relegated when couples are establishing a joint identity. We have already referred to those who find it difficult to give up 'playing the field' and continue to behave as if they are still single. Ordinary friendships and activities outside the marriage can also cause tension if they take no account of marital commitments, as another young woman found out:

'Christopher got this money and spent it on a holiday skiing. I was put out, but not drastically put out. But then, afterwards, I learned that the other members of the party had accepted him as a bachelor and he had gone along with that.'

Becoming a couple takes time; commitment has to be made to a joint identity.

Some people, brought up in the expectation of forging a career and getting near the top if not right to the top in their profession, may be deeply committed to their work. (These days people are often less committed to the actual firm they work for than in the past. The greater size of many firms, and the social and spatial distance between owners and workers or top managers and lower managers, do not promote the loyalties and identifications that were once part of many people's working life.) But again there need be no problem in the marriage if the partner is equally committed to and supports the career climb. In this type of marriage there is little blurring of roles. Usually it is the husband who is committed to his career and to increasing his earning capacity, and who is dependent upon his wife for most if not all of the child care and domestic responsibilities, organization, routine, style and comfort. The wife, dependent on her husband's increasing earnings, is committed to the work of home-making for him and their children. However, as women increasingly go out to work the possibility of conflicting loyalties becomes stronger. We shall return to this issue in Chapter 6.

In many marriages the commitment to children can at times be in conflict with the earlier commitment to the partner. Difficult choices have to be made between opposing needs. There may be less conflict for those people whose underlying commitment in marriage is to parenting rather than partnering. Partnering for them is a means to the end of parenting. Such couples are often recognized by the loss of their first names: they become Mummy and Daddy to one another as well as to the children.

However much babies are wanted, and however firm the commitment to them may be, partners can feel deserted by each other when most in need of help and support. Husbands may resent the exclusive nature of the nursing couple – mother and baby apparently absorbed only in each other – and long to be included. Wives, becoming less absorbed as babies become more clearly their own persons, but often remaining tied, tired or bored by the demands of toddlers, perhaps feeling lonely and lacking enough external stimulus, may similarly find themselves resenting and envying what they see as their husbands' 'freedom' of action.

Few of us are immune from envy. Envy between the sexes is so common that we could say it is inevitable – even natural. People who can allow themselves to know about their envy at least give themselves a chance of attempting to handle it relatively wisely. Those less in touch with the feeling, or unconsciously consumed by repressed but unmitigated envy from their own infancy, are often in trouble when a real baby is part of the married scene. For a person who has been severely deprived in early childhood, envy of the baby who is receiving all the care that was and still is so much wanted can feel intolerable.

Whether conscious or not of their own envy, the people in the most difficulty are those who feel they have been born the wrong sex – suspicious, or even quite clear, that their parents desperately wanted them to be the boy or girl they were not. They can never realize the parental aspiration other than in a superficial way, and they are left not only with the envy of the sex they were meant to be, but also unable to enjoy the sex which they are and the advantages which pertain to it.

Largely preoccupied by a sense of not being able to win, they have little sense of commitment to themselves, let alone to a person of the opposite sex. With no experience of being accepted for who and what they were and are, it is hard for them in their turn to accept the other for what he or she is, or is becoming. Most probably, having married their own problem in their unconscious choice of partner – one who also disappoints – it will be particularly difficult for them to convert this inevitably disappointing choice into conscious commitment.

Sometimes commitments are made to those outside marriage in order to buttress a wavering commitment to the self. A parent, hobby, friend, lover, child or job may be introduced to provide a buffer against claims from the partner which threaten to overwhelm the self. Such triangular set-ups provide a means of regulating distance in a marriage, and may represent a bid to retain freedom and independence. The interactive nature of marriage means that such actions can have escalating effects. The more one partner backs off, the more the other may be impelled to pursue. Pursuit encourages further retreat, and so a vicious spiral is established which can destabilize a relationship.

Finding an acceptable balance between closeness and distance is, as we have said, an age-old relationship conundrum. Kahlil Gibran's Prophet captured the paradox with his use of imagery:

> *Sing and dance together and be joyous, but let each one of you be alone,*
> *Even as the strings of the lute are alone though*
>   *they quiver with the same music.*

> *And stand together yet not too near together:*
> *For the pillars of the temple stand apart,*
> *And the oak tree and the cypress grow not in*
>   *each others' shadow.*

The same oppositional balance is expressed in more prosaic language by two men who each described one of the two polarities:

'I've always disliked the idea of couples when they're like Siamese twins, like it's always "Charlie and Kate", and it's never one alone. If people see Charlie on his own they say "Where's Kate?", and vice versa. I've never liked that approach.'

'We look at other couples where you see the man with his hobbies and his pint, and the wife has her friends and bingo. Although they live together and have children they don't seem to be a couple, they just seem to be two people who do their own thing. We don't want to fall into that situation. That would be terrible.'

Life is complex when partners are bidding for marriage and family life as well as for themselves. We could say that the conflict in any modern marriage is between the needs of self, the needs of the partnership (each partner wanting to support the other, but refusing to be swamped by or subjugated to the other), the needs of children, the needs of the family as a group and the needs of those outside the family. There is plenty of scope for conflicting commitments. With the options now open to couples, commitments and covenants will need to be renegotiated and re-formulated many times in the course of a lifetime as family groups move through different stages. An ability to communicate is essential in this process. There must be a dialogue in marriage. We go on now to look at the importance of the dialogue, and the problems which can occur when communication breaks down.

5. *Intercourse*

THICK SKINS AND THIN SKINS

Intercourse, whether mental or physical, requires penetration. One person's idea can influence and spark off a better idea in another, and through the interchange something can be created which is more useful than either could achieve alone. Words, smiles, laughs and hugs can warm the heart of another. Bodies can invite or offer penetration and so create an embryo. Creation through entry and reception sounds so easy, but . . .

Words and bodies can repel as well as attract. They can chill and starve as well as warm and nourish. They can do both at the same time. Voice, eyes, mouth and posture can contradict the actual verbal message. Stony, glassy eyes can contradict smiling mouths. Smiles can also be chilly, just as words can bite and sneer. Apparently warming hugs can be most ungiving and greedily grasping for the self. And bodies can fail to respond to the dictates of the conscious mind. Emotions, and particularly conflicting emotions, are powerful in their ascendance over intellect and they may display themselves more accurately through the body than through words. Feelings that have been firmly repressed, near the surface yet still not sufficiently available to be formed into words, can express themselves through bodily symptoms; if these feelings relate to permeability, they may well be expressed on the skin – rashes, blotches, spots and boils – and become boundary symptoms.

Most people identify coldness with hostility and deprivation; warmth with friendliness, nourishment, closeness and intimacy. Yet no one can tolerate too much intimacy. The closer we allow ourselves to get to another, the more we are affected and influenced both consciously and unconsciously through the projective system of defence we described in the last two chapters. We need to move away as well as towards. Some people can never

79

dare to move closer because of the inevitable withdrawal that must follow; the prospect feels too chilly by contrast.

Finding a comfortable emotional distance, encouraging and allowing some penetration without being taken over completely, is the task of all relationships. A major factor in maintaining relationships is the measure of success people have in finding a mutually comfortable distance.

In writing of the 'sediment' of aversion and hostility which exists in every intimate relationship, even the most loving, Freud quoted Schopenhauer's famous simile of the freezing porcupines:

> A company of porcupines crowded themselves together one cold winter's day so as to profit from one another's warmth and so save themselves from being frozen to death. But soon they felt one another's quills, which induced them to separate again. And now, when the need for warmth brought them nearer together again, the second evil arose once more. So they were driven backwards and forwards from one trouble to the other, until they had discovered a mean distance at which they could tolerably exist.[1]

Some people's quills are longer than those of others. Some people have thick skins, others have thin ones and are more easily hurt. There is no correct distance, although as Rilke said, 'A good marriage is that which appoints the other as guardian of his solitude.' But just as some marriages can at times feel suffocating, so they may at others feel uncomfortably distant. As Byng-Hall has written, 'Spouses need to know and heed these signs.' He described an adequate marriage as having periods of intimacy interspersed with periods of autonomy for both partners, who, at the same time, do not allow the relationship to become too tenuous and know that the other will be there when needed.[2]

Let us look in more detail at the difficulties inherent for everyone in appropriate penetration and then at the problems that can arise in marriage when these are of an extreme nature. We consider these difficulties in relation firstly to verbal and bodily intercourse 'out of bed' and, secondly, verbal, bodily and sexual intercourse 'in bed'.

OUT OF BED

Even when our conscious feelings are not in a state of conflict, it is difficult to portray them relatively accurately in words, but it is much more so when they are. Probably, when our feelings are consistent, the words, perhaps stumbling and inadequate, matter less. We can be trite or clumsy in our choice of words, but the strength of feeling is adequately conveyed. Some people are better than others in the use of words, but for some feelings, words always seem grossly inadequate. Sometimes, with the best of intentions, the words do not come out quite right. And it is difficult to know how they will be heard. How thick or thin is the other's skin? A simple word which to one person is relatively neutral can be emotive dynamite to another. Similarly, some words which are meant to stir can leave others unmoved.

In Chapter 3 we spoke of the importance of being able to signal, and of the influence of early experiences in acquiring confidence that signals will be seen or heard and then responded to. Is it safe to ask directly? If we cannot ask directly, if we cannot risk a 'No', do we have to scream for what we want? Or do we use stealth to obtain it? Perhaps 'Thank you' and 'Sorry', so easy to say to a stranger, are two of the most difficult words to say to our nearest and dearest. If some words are emotionally difficult to form – stay like stones in the throat – a verbal diarrhoea by which every thought and feeling has to be expelled forthwith can be equally uncommunicative. It induces others to 'shut off' and refuse further penetration. It also allows the diarrhoetic person no time for listening or taking in from the other.

How difficult it is to listen to others! Perhaps it is one of the most difficult things in life. Most of us value a good listener. But in the business of everyday life, in our self-absorption which at times takes over, the request for attention may feel intrusive just when we do not want to be intruded upon. And what if the request for attention conflicts with our own similar need, as in the incident we described in Chapter 1 under 'Babies and Bathwater', where both partners were tired and needed recognition before they could meet the similar need in the other. Who can be allowed to come first? Will I have a good enough share of time if I allow myself to listen first and tell second? Are the signals clear? Is my attention really needed at this moment, or can it wait? Do I have to permit penetration *now*?

And when our partners are not good with words, can we notice the communications made by the body? Some people express more of their feelings through their eyes, their hands or their whole posture than through their words. Different people make more use of one sense than another: they may see more than they hear; or they may feel more than they see, even though they have sight.

June and Robert Braithwaite complained of their inability to communicate. June described the depth of her frustration when she could not get Robert to respond to her words. She felt guilty about nagging but driven to do so. When nagging failed, her frustration reached a pitch in which she screamed and threw objects round the house. Would nothing less than a scream or a thrown object penetrate him?

Words were important to her. She liked them, read a lot, and in unemotional situations could use them well. She described herself as introspective, and when not totally frustrated she could analyse much of her behaviour and choose what she would or would not say. She now wondered if she and Robert had ever communicated properly. She thought they had started from different points, although she had wanted to marry him after only a few meetings because he 'felt good to be with'. Robert had been attracted to her 'lively mind', feeling himself inadequate with words. Then he had valued her ability to express things for them both. Now he said he found it difficult to show his feelings, but he clearly experienced the world through his senses, particularly touch. He wanted to touch June more than she wanted to be touched and he was bitterly upset that June was rejecting him sexually. She thought he was just 'using' her in bed. Without being aware of it, he punished her for this deeply felt bodily rejection in bed by withdrawing his body out of bed. When not working, he was playing sport, busy with his hands or training his dog. He spoke lovingly of the dog and his words were most explicit when he explained how he understood its 'learning by association'. He did a lot for the children, warmed and warming in his need to hold and touch them. He could never understand why June became so irritated by his 'never reading the directions'. She could not understand that he preferred to work things out for himself 'by the feel'. What he experienced through his hands made more sense to him than written words of instruction.

Although Robert used his body more than words to communicate, he failed to recognize June's bodily communications when her words failed to penetrate him. Even the violent messages, when she threw things round the room, went unheeded. She was the 'mad' one, rather than a person trying to get him to hear. When she cried in the first therapeutic session, he could not move over to comfort her and was surprised when the therapist drew attention to this strong communication which he had ignored.

In this first session she demonstrated how she nagged him and went on and on trying to get the response she wanted. At one point he corrected her too easily made assumption and then pointed out to the therapist that he had shown his feelings: his voice had risen because her remarks had made him angry. 'You've seen I'm cross, haven't you?' he asked. His anger had been just barely visible to a carefully watching eye. At the end of the session, June Braithwaite said she had found it useful; she had not needed to become hysterical, and he had not been able to leave and disappear into the kitchen.

Like many previous philosophers and psychologists, Jung devised a typology to distinguish personality types, the characteristic ways in which different people use their minds and react to their environment.[3] First he distinguished the extroverted person from the introverted one – attitude types, as he called them. The extrovert relates strongly to the world about him, to things outside himself and to other people. He seeks less of his own company and moves more towards others than away from them. He can be uncomfortable, even distressed if the world is too bare or temporarily unpeopled. He may well ask for space for himself, but always space in relation to another. He is often a practical person. In contrast, the introverted person is concerned with the space between people and objects. He seeks out and moves into gaps. A lot of the time he needs space just for himself, to move on his own. More often his thoughts, feelings and responses centre on his inner world, his imagery and on understanding phenomena both inside and outside himself.

No one is totally of one type or the other. Many primarily introverted people can deal with the outside world when required, just as many extroverts can deal with ideas when this is needed. Jung's distinction drew attention to whether a person relates predominantly to others and less to the self or vice versa.

Secondly, he distinguished between four different 'function types', based on the way people perceive and judge the world. Related to perception were two strongly contrasting ways of taking in and becoming aware of what was happening. The first was through the five senses. The second was by intuition, a much less conscious process than sensation. In this second case a person was less aware of the actual stimulus but quickly in tune with his own associations and what he could 'read between the lines'. The two other main functions concerned contrasting ways of judging and ordering these perceptions. First, there was thinking: a logical, conscious and often impersonal process. Second, there was feeling, the word used not in the conventional sense, but to describe a much less consciously formulated process of appreciation and subjective valuation.

These four functions can be combined in one of four ways:

sensing and thinking
sensing and feeling
intuition and thinking
intuition and feeling

They can also be combined with extroverted or introverted attitude types thus making eight combinations in all. So with one of the four functions normally predominant over the other three we can speak of a sensate, intuitive, thinking or feeling type of person, who can be either extroverted or introverted. These combinations produce very different types of personality, and conflict can easily occur when people are using opposite ways of perceiving and making judgements.

Just as people show a preference for one way of perceiving and one way of making judgements, they also, said Jung, show a preference between the processes of perceiving and judging. Some people keep their mind more open to further perceptions and are slow to judge. Others arrive at verdicts much more quickly. So we can often distinguish between people who live their life as it happens and those who run their lives.

The predominant use of one function rather than another is not, said Jung, to be despised. Just as a ship needs a captain, so too does the individual need a governing principle. If, for example, two perceptive functions are of equal weight, they tend to interfere with and jam each other. One perceptive and one judging process can develop side by side, provided one remains subordinate and auxiliary to the other. Thus a primary perceptive function can be supported by an auxiliary judging process and vice versa, but thinking and feeling can never support each other, nor can sensation and intuition.

Clearly it is easier to assess the predominant function used by an extrovert than that used by an introvert, just because the extrovert likes immediate communication. But it is important not to rush into too neat or speedy a conclusion about another person's main and natural form of mental functioning. In an over-determined upbringing and education, a child or young person can be forced into a way of using their mind antithetical to their own natural bias. People functioning on an imposed bias may be severely handicapped when what they think is expected of them is at some level distonic to their whole being.

Obviously this typology has immense implications for educational methods, for communication generally, and for choice of marriage partner. As we described in Chapter 3, some people base their marriage on identification, others on complementarity. They may marry an extroverted intuitive-thinking type like themselves, or an introverted sensation-feeling type quite unlike themselves. The complementary combination may well be more creative eventually, but more difficult to handle in the process of communication and working out how much space a couple ask of and can offer to each other.

Robert Braithwaite soon emerged strongly as a sensation type with feeling as his auxiliary function. At the time we first met him his limited confidence in himself had been further undermined by June Braithwaite's derision of his way of 'going on'. Just because she used many more words, he thought of her as a thinking type. But in Jung's terms she was an intuitive-feeling type. As she said when talking about their courtship, 'I wanted to marry him because I felt good with him. I can't explain it any further.' Her perception was not clearly defined by sensations and she made a value-judgement not based on a logical process. Robert also made value-judgements, but based these judgements on actual sensations.

Despite her normal command over words, June Braithwaite found it difficult to ask in ways that were likely to obtain for her what she wanted. Instead of asking Robert to spend more time with her at the weekends, she blamed him for being absent when something quite minor happened to one of the children.

Blaming the other is a common phenomenon and we all resort to it at times, whether justified or not. Those who blame most and ask least – 'You never do anything for me', 'You never take me out' – are usually very vulnerable, deprived people with little basic trust that others will or can be helpful. Continued blame is often a communication of despair. This despair frequently relates back to early experiences when adults were literally more powerful than children and were therefore blamed by those children for some of the awful things, real or imaginary, that happened to them. Those who perpetually blame others often find attachment very difficult but are frightened of separating and being alone. They want other people to come close, but are petrified when closeness is offered. In their ambivalence, their way of asking often ensures that they do not get the closeness they say they want.

In the last chapter we described the defence of splitting between the anger and the yearning aroused by the absence of the needed, safe figure. An adult's constant blaming of another can also be heard as the angry protest of the deprived internal infant within that adult body, and when it turns to whining, may also serve to express the yearning and become an attempt to control the whereabouts of the other. Invariably it is an ineffective communication as it antagonizes and also leaves the subject not knowing whether help would otherwise have been offered spontaneously.

Those who constantly blame others put the cause of everything they do not like outside themselves. They often remain in a state of despair that the world at large and their nearest friends and relatives treat them so badly. The split in the mind, formed so early in their lives, becomes a predominant defence against feeling and knowing more about themselves.

When both partners in a marriage consistently blame the other and suffer from the accompanying underlying despair, the marriage is likely to be in difficulties from the beginning. In the rows and fights which ensue, the pot calls the kettle black. The continued process is often accentuated by disappointment in the other because of an earlier idealization. At the age when such a split is formed, such is the yearning for the food, comfort, holding and love which are withheld that the good becomes idealized. With the smallest fall from grace, it is quickly turned into badness. In adult years, help from the partner never feels quite sufficient and, therefore, cannot be appreciated. All that is required must be offered and, if it is not *all*, it is felt to be useless.

Sometimes when two such people marry, they maintain a loving, close relationship by projecting all the blame into the outside world. As a couple, they appear as 'babes in the wood', helpless and hopeless together as they would be on their own, beset by the awfulness of everyone else.

Other people, with a mountain of blame in their inner world which they are afraid to express, may use their partner to do this for them. One partner then blames, blames, and blames again both inside and outside the marriage. The other, frightened of a similar propensity, consciously abhors what becomes so tedious, but unconsciously fuels the fury and whine because of the need to keep in touch with the repudiated blaming, whining self. Those who have been immensely blamed, or felt they were blamed, may well marry a blaming partner. If they can become less blamed, they will then have resolved something important for themselves.

Things had gone seriously wrong for Derek Young when his younger brother ran out into the road, was hit by a car, and suffered severe brain damage from which he never recovered, spending the rest of his life as a vegetable in a long-stay hospital. Derek's father never recovered from this loss and refused to acknowledge the younger child's previous or continued existence. Derek remained confused. He had vague memories of a brother who apparently did not exist any more. He was led to believe there never had been a brother. He could not make it out, nor could he trust his own memory.

At the time his brother was injured and disappeared, the five-year-old Derek was still of an age when thinking is often magical in quality and wrong connections can be made. Somewhere in his mind was a misconnection that his anger with his brother had actually killed him. Just before the accident, he had snatched his favourite toy from his brother and had been stopped by his mother from hitting him over the head. The immediate thought that his anger had killed his brother was so terrible that he repressed it; his loss of memory abetted his father's dismissal of the injured child.

Derek grew up to be a careful young man, never prizing any possession too much and desperately afraid of making a mistake. Mis-spoken words were too dangerous. He trained and practised as a solicitor, was excessively conscientious, and always warned his clients, as he warned himself, that any ill-thought out actions could spell disaster of some unspecified kind. Stoically he put up with the complaints of his wife, Elsie. Despite his meeting so many of her demands on his time and attention, she often complained about and blamed him for his inattentiveness. There was much truth in this accusation, as he remained obsessed by his inner confusion and disturbing half-memories. He was a bad listener.

In therapy he was helped to recall what had been so bothering to him and illogically connected. With the safety and containment of the therapy behind him, he dared (but still unconsciously) to make a mistake in his work. He succeeded in no uncertain terms. It was a bad mistake. He expected to be sacked. But no, it turned out to be a most therapeutic mistake. The partners of his firm acknowledged that the back-up had not been sufficient. The whole firm, working as a team, set about rectifying his mistake. Even bad mistakes, he learned, could be retrieved. Even more amazing, Elsie, who had been getting in touch with her previously repudiated strengths, stopped complaining for the day. Instead of telephoning him at work to blame or to demand attention for herself, she responded to the emergency and visited the office with soup and sandwiches to keep them all going through the evening.

Many books of advice assure people that once they start communicating properly, all their troubles will be over. This is easier said than done. People can go on communicating for hours on end, but if they are not talking about the really important issue, the time is not well spent. Often what needs to be communicated is not fully conscious. One constant theme often underlies a series of quarrels or rows on seemingly different issues. At one level, Bob and Joan Halton rowed about his old car and his mother. At a deeper level, they rowed about greed – guilt about greed and protection from supposedly greedy women.

At one level, June Braithwaite attacked Robert about the time he spent away from home and what he did and did not do for the children. The frustration he caused her was the keynote of every one-sided altercation. Yet much of her frustration was of her own making and within herself. Her father had expected excessively high standards of her as a child – better deportment, better table manners and better school reports – all of which she felt she could never attain.

She projected a fused image of her father and mother on to Robert. He became the rejecting father who never helped her, while at the same time she asked him to be mother and take over. When he did take over, his touching, hugging care of the children, which they adored, made her feel even more inadequate.

Robert was one of a large family. As a child he had felt very unnoticed, lost in the middle between older and younger children. He soon learned to find solace on his own out of doors. He had wanted to be more noticed as a child. June, too, had wanted to be noticed for herself and not just for failing to attain impossibly high standards. We could say that most of their quarrels were about notice – who noticed whom and in connection with what.

In their defensive exchanges, they ceased to value what had first so attracted them to each other. June's having noticed him when they first met and her ability to put things into words now became unbearable to Robert. She took too much notice of his comings and goings and her sharp words pierced his skin (not as thick as she supposed) through to the heart. His once quiet, undemanding ease now felt to her a lack of response, a rejecting casual indifference.

Some couples, highly intelligent and normally with a good command over words, manage to keep themselves endlessly but unknowingly confused. They may have many detailed conversations without realizing that each has attributed a different meaning to the 'it' or the 'that' they are talking about. They continue to converse at cross purposes and wonder why their numerous conversations never seem to get anywhere or resolve any disagreement. It seems that there is an underlying need to keep things private and undisturbed by the other – a refusal to allow penetration. People who fall into this habit often have a weak sense of identity and have felt very taken over as children, not allowed their own thoughts and feelings, nor to be themselves. Unconsciously they create a smokescreen of confusion as a defence against the fear of being taken over.

Other ineffective communicators fail to mention what 'it' actually is because they still carry an infantile illusion of being able to fuse with another – an unconscious belief, wish or rueful hope that one person can get inside the mind of another. They expect a loved one to understand without first being told; perfect, intuitive empathy is anticipated.

Brenda Acton, a seemingly competent and well-organized person, had a habit of talking about various events in her life as if other people had prior knowledge of the circumstances leading up to these events. It always sounded as if one should have known, had been told before and was rather foolish to have forgotten. She complained bitterly about her husband being so confused and his always forgetting what she had told him without having any insight into her own ability to confuse him and other people. But as a child she had many times been wrested (as it felt to her) from her known environment into some strange place, leaving her totally confused. Once she suddenly landed up in hospital for what was not an emergency; several times she had found herself in a new home; and on one occasion she had arrived in another country with a new 'father' – all without warning or previous explanation. All big changes in her young life had been suddenly thrust upon her.

She had experienced her mother as a distant figure who at times just grabbed her and moved her about, but she had not had the physical and emotional closeness that she craved and needed. In her attempt to get closer to her mother she had unknowingly identified with the mother's way of not explaining anything. Then, in her attempt to experience more closeness to her husband and to drive him to understand what she felt like but could not make conscious or put into words, she did to him what had been done to her. She left him confused, just as she had been left confused. This is a common phenomenon. When words and memories fail, enactments take over as attempts at communication.

Frustration with the ineffectiveness of words lies behind a lot of physical violence. It may seem odd to think of battering as an attempt to get close. But battering, like blaming, can serve the expression of opposing feelings. Fury at the behaviour of the other, or at what the other symbolizes, can be a desperate attempt to get physically and emotionally closer by sharing the experience of what it is like to be battered. Even if we find it difficult to imagine the strength of feeling behind this ambivalence, most of us can recall or visualize the ambivalence in a parent's action when given a 'friendly cuff', or when threatened with a poised hand and a laughing voice. Some severely neglected children do at times actually value a cuff, a blow or a kick. Their sad reasoning goes that at least they are noticed when hit, and this is better than what otherwise feels like oblivion. In a family in which 'asking' is always done by a threatening fist, and physical violence is the usual means of expressing ill-temper or frustration, the difference between welfare and ill-fare is the strength of the blow rather than the fact that it happened.

As we have seen, conscious or unconscious envy of what the other is, or has, underlies much of the fury and frustration which is expressed in physical violence. Envy is one of the strongest antidotes to love and has its roots in the innate and primitive anger and anxiety of infancy. When the fury in the bedevilled infant is not constantly mediated by proper care, comfort and attention, it festers and finds expression in later life. Anything which symbolizes the early lack of care can strengthen or pierce the defences. With adult weight behind uncontrolled infantile panic, the flailing arm strikes and damages.

Christopher Watts could not understand why he had attacked his wife. The unpredictability and inexplicability of his action added to his terror as well as to hers. The world 'went blank', he said. 'Is my violence akin to madness?' he asked his therapist. He talked of his harsh, unsympathetic upbringing in which his often drunken father physically abused his wife and children. After leaving school he had been unable to settle, had wandered from place to place and had eventually landed up in Borstal, where his crimes had given him a reputation for toughness and ruthlessness which he had felt compelled to live up to (although at the same time hating it and himself). In therapy some of the sources of his rage were exposed, particularly the lack of love within the alternating violence and apathy of the parenting he had received. The link between his emerging depression and his violent behaviour, the latter defending him from the former, made sense to him. He became very depressed for some time before he could reassess himself, start to use his considerable abilities and begin courting his wife again.

It was never clear exactly what in his wife's behaviour had felt so rejecting and triggered off his attack on her, but the attack had occurred shortly after the birth of their first child. It may well have related to his envy of the nursing pair and the demand he experienced to be a *good* father. He had little conviction that he could fulfil this role properly, his own experience of being fathered having been so grossly inadequate.

He felt only shame about what had happened. There had been no conscious pleasure for him in the attack. Some violence is, of course, sheer unadulterated sadism with an accompanying orgiastic delight in hurting and harming. However perverse or abhorrent this may be, it is important to remember that we all have a sadistic capacity and there are not many people so out of touch with the darker, deeper aspects of their human nature that they have never indulged a sadistic fantasy. Masochism is the other side of the coin, the victim's pleasure in the pain and humiliation heaped upon him often remaining unconscious. Masochism is a defence against unacknowledged sadism and masochists will, in the terms of the unconscious 'fit' between partners, tend to marry not necessarily a conscious sadist, but often one who helps them to maintain a masochistic role. It is usually noticeable that when a masochist has for years felt hard done by, often over-controlled by their partner, and then for some reason the tables are turned, he or she metes out punishment as if this has to go on for the same length of time that the masochist's suffering was endured.

Emily Tranter remained silently resentful of her husband's control of money and all major decisions for over fifteen years. When at last she gained some independence by taking a job which gave her some income of her own, she suddenly put her foot down. No, she was not going along with his decision as to how they should spend their holiday. She heaped her scorn on what became his tentatively offered ideas. Within two years a fine-looking, commanding man had become a shadow of his former self. In no way had he been consciously sadistic over the earlier years, but he had a deep fear of women who took over, as his mother had done. Quite unconsciously he had punished his wife instead of his mother and protected himself from bossy women by holding the marital reigns so tightly. When the coin flipped over, it seemed as if the punishment would be never-ending.

A constant need to control other people normally arises from deep insecurity and a lack of confidence in the self – a fear of being left and disbelief in the self being lovable. Phillip Tranter controlled through words and strongly expressed beliefs which were difficult to counter. Physical violence is also a means of trying to keep control, sometimes a conscious coercion to get others to obey through fear. There are other coercive techniques. Blackmail is one. A suicidal gesture is another, often unconsciously made when help is likely to be at hand. Although gestures can misfire and some serious suicide attempts fail (it is not always easy to distinguish between the gesture and the serious attempt), both acts are expressions of immense aggression and can leave behind a trail of guilt and remorse. Sometimes they succeed in pressuring others to come to heel.

Constant illness and helplessness also control. Derek Young was exceptionally controlled in his demeanour and general behaviour, unconsciously fearing another disaster like the loss of his brother if he did not exercise sufficient control. He chose a dependent wife in Elsie, who further controlled him by her ailments and excessive demands. June Braithwaite attempted to control Robert Braithwaite, but failed. In both these marriages the sexual intercourse was unsatisfactory for one or both partners. The control got into bed with them. Intercourse in bed normally reflects intercourse out of bed.

IN BED

Much of what we have written about verbal intercourse is relevant to the understanding of problems in sexual intercourse. People afraid of verbal penetration are often afraid of sexual penetration. Those who have difficulty in sustaining and carrying things through out of bed may also be premature ejaculators in bed. Inveterate controllers are rarely adequate as physical lovers, unable to let go or risk too much excitement. People who can never dare to move close because of the inevitable withdrawal afterwards may experience little sexual desire. Sexual intercourse epitomizes intimacy and closeness and, therefore, accentuates the actuality of separation in the aftermath. At an unconscious level, distaste, lack of desire or avoidance of bodily intimacy may be used as a defence against the experience of ultimate aloneness which can follow the fusion of intercourse. When sexual intercourse does take place, the partner is often chided for turning over or away, sometimes even in sleep. Or the complaint is made of 'just being used'.

Similarly, those who cannot bear to know about differences between people out of bed, and whose marriage is based more on identification than complementarity, can be disturbed by actual bodily differences which cannot be ignored in bed.

In the reflection of what is going on out of bed, people with relatively well-integrated personalities find that their sexual intercourse over the years represents a variety of feelings and moods. They can enjoy to varying extents exciting sex, passionate sex, lazy sex, warm and comforting sex, at times even angry or disgruntled sex, and then, perhaps, forgiving sex. Forgiveness and atonement may be expressed through the act when feelings are starting to move that way, but the words still too difficult to articulate.

People whose sexual behaviour is at total variance with their previous mood – the most exciting and passionate sex following the most horrendous and enraged row – are demonstrating a split or lack of integration in their personality. If they go into therapy, they may be disappointed to find that while their marriage is improving or more comfortable generally, sex has 'gone off' as it starts to become more variable and follow their actual mood. The mood by this time may be more depressed, as they start to look at their own problems as opposed to those of their partner. However, the analytic therapist is pleased by this sign of increasing integration and hopeful that sex will come back to life as the couple move through the depression and the marriage improves.

Expression through and enjoyment of bodily closeness and sexual inter-course is much influenced by early blueprints and, therefore, often reflects emotional development. We can say that sexual delight, or the lack of it, is the direct heir of infancy. People who as babies were handled with love and delight, whose perfect little bodies were so much admired, and who did not acquire 'hang-ups' from later unfortunate experiences, do not seem to have problems with sexual intercourse. They have less need of instruction manuals and can follow their instincts and the dictates of their heart. Those who have learnt of the otherness of the other can communicate bodily, or with words, what pleases and what does not.

People whose parents or early carers have not enjoyed contact with infant bodies nor valued their bodily functions may find it difficult to enjoy either their own body and its sensations or the body of another. If sharing between mother and baby was minimal, the baby held too tightly and not allowed to play with breast or bottle, pleasing the self by masturbation may give more satisfaction than intercourse and pleasure given by another, as it may if the baby was left too much on its own, the bottle propped up against the pillow.

People who have been held awkwardly may in their turn be stiff, ashamed of nudity or partial nudity, or carry a fantasy that if only the scene were properly set, rosy lights dimly aglow, all would come right. The agent has to be external and never within themselves. They cannot imagine any delight in a tumble of ungainly bodies nor can they accept the fact that the sexual act is not graceful. Usually they have few if any memories of being comforted on a lap, tossed in the air by their father (why do men toss babies and women so rarely?), delicious bathing times with games and squeals of delight, and well-earned praise and parental pleasure when they excreted in nappy or pot. More often the memory is of the displeasure that their body and its excretions caused. Because the genital organ is also the urinary one, or adjacent to it, attitudes inculcated in respect of urination can get displaced on to sex. Persistent bedwetters or soilers, for whatever reason, physical or psychological, may well have problems in their later adult sexual performance.

Some people feel they have been put off sex by a parent's clear disgust. The message may be communicated by direct remark or innuendo: 'Sex is dirty', 'I have to put up with your father', or 'It never did anything for me.' But these attitudes to sex are often a reflection of attitudes to bodies generally, indicating the lack of joy in body experienced many years before.

Some mothers can enjoy and care well for a baby in arms, but are disturbed by and neglectful of a toddler who starts to express independence and move away as well as towards. The rejection of the newly mobile toddler may be accentuated if another baby is born at this time. For such a toddler the sudden loss of the early comfort can leave a continued yearning for it and lack of satisfaction in activities related to later developmental stages. In later life the actual genital act may mean very little – a mere sideshow. Intercourse may be performed occasionally or specifically for reproduction, but continued cuddling and bodily warmth from another is what gives the real satisfaction.

Breasts may be more sensuous than bottoms for people who either experienced great satisfaction at their mother's breast or never had enough of it. Bottoms may be more or less sensuous to those whose old preoccupations centred on anal functions. There may have been problems of mastery, of control, of appropriate letting go; or an early refusal to let go as resistance to an over-persistent potty-training parent.

Repression is one of the most influential enemies of sexual desire. Strong repression of one emotion often succeeds inadvertently in suppressing the desire as well. When, for example, a previously repressed anger comes back into consciousness and it becomes safer for a person to acknowledge his hostility, desire is also freed. Clive Greenacre was not only put out when his agoraphobic wife started to express her anger about his callous behaviour, but also amazed by the sexual demands she then started to make on him. Previously he had blamed her for the lack of sexual satisfaction she gave him, experiencing her as semi-frigid and totally unexciting. But just as he had used her agoraphobia as a defence against having to know about his need to find her safely where he had left her, so too did her lack of sexual response defend him from knowing about his need to keep her under his control. As she became more sexually active – to him, frighteningly so – he became seriously disturbed about whether he could keep up with her. An erection two nights running was now required. And then he became even more worried about what she might get up to with a lover. Previously he had had no worry about her possible infidelity or that she might leave him for a more effective performer. Needless to say, her new-found potency gave rise to deep misgivings about his own sexual adequacy.

Problems of sexual intercourse are as interactive at an unconscious level as some of a couple's intercourse out of bed. The problem, whether it be vaginismus (painful contraction of the vaginal muscles) in the woman or failure to obtain an erection by the man, can be complained about and used as a defence against recognizing the problem in the self. Treatment for a sexual problem in one partner is rarely successful, or if it first appears so when some mental block is eased, results in the exposure of the problem in the other. Some people faithfully hang on to their problem, sabotaging help when unconsciously they experience their partner as more vulnerable than themselves and in need of protection. Similarly, some couples assiduously hang on to a sexual problem as a defence against facing up to a much wider problem in their marriage.

Many sexual problems are treated these days primarily by educational or instructive methods, which can be very effective. After a full history is taken, physical examination performed and a round-table discussion held in which cause and effect may be established, old myths abolished, points of ignorance removed, and communication between the partners opened up, the couple are introduced to the idea of learning more about each other's sensual responses generally. They are instructed in 'pleasuring' or 'sensate focus', whereby in the privacy of their own bedroom they have to experiment with handling, fondling, and massaging their partner with the purpose of learning what gives most pleasure to the other and to the self. They are told to avoid the genital area. For some people this is literally the first time they have thought about and felt sensual responses in their own body. After further round-table discussions of their progress, pleasuring is then extended to the genital area before they are encouraged to attempt intercourse, with different recommendations for particular problems.

Although attention is given in the discussions to underlying emotional problems such as we have described in this chapter, some people's emotional 'blocks' do not shift in this setting. In the jargon it is said that they cannot even get on the Masters and Johnson 'ski-slope', let alone start down it. (Masters and Johnson were the innovators of the above type of treatment, following eleven years of detailed research into human sexual functioning).[4] At the discussions, time is given to cause and effect, but this is mainly at a conscious level. For example, some premature ejaculation is patterned by early courting habits – too many rushed exchanges in the back of a car – or by early experiences with prostitutes when the faster the customer performs, the more the prostitute is pleased. People usually start to feel better about a problem when they have some explanation for it, but hang-ups relating to very early patterns of relating between mother and baby which we have been describing may not come to light within the time normally allowed for this type of treatment. Sometimes a deeper, analytic therapy may be required before people can use instruction.

When parents have implicitly forbidden their otherwise relatively mature children to be fully sexual creatures, there can be enormous value in being given permission by an authoritative therapist to have and enjoy sex. But when permissive or instructional therapy is needed, the interesting question is why people remain so ignorant about their bodies and potential sexuality when there are so many relevant books on the market, when sex education is provided in schools and when many glossy magazines promote the virtue and necessity of orgasm. Friedman, writing about the work done by a group of doctors in Family Planning Clinics with women who had been unable to consummate their marriage, typified certain syndromes by reference to myths.[5] (Psychoanalysis shows that many legends and fairy stories owe their continued appeal to their 'artful representation' of common unconscious fantasies related to early stages of psychological development.)

One group of wives were called 'Sleeping Beauties'. They were in one sense still asleep and unable to know about their sexual organs, using the defence of not knowing against an anxiety aroused by the prospect of copulation. Sometimes they complained about their vagina being too small. They often suffered from vaginismus, but they invariably praised their husbands for being 'exceptionally kind', passive, totally understanding and 'so good as not to bother me'.

Another group, 'Gentling Brünnhildes', aggressive, masculine women, had strong competitive feelings towards men, but at another level desperately wanted to be overpowered and mastered as Brünnhilde, it will be remembered, was eventually mastered by Siegfried. These women were often sweetly reasonable, but used their vaginal muscles to fight their husbands and were afraid of men who might make demands on them.

Brünnhildes often held a persistent attachment to their fathers or mothers and their aggressiveness towards men was a means of protecting this tie.

A third group were the 'Queen Bees', virgin wives and often virgin mothers who had in the past persuaded a doctor to administer artificial insemination because of their husband's impotence. Less consciously, their desire was for a baby to be given to them by a symbolic mother (the female doctor). Often their request for help was for further insemination and not to treat the actual sexual problem. Non-consummation is one obvious cause of infertility, but some fertility clinics do not always question the assumed fact and frequency of intercourse.

Severe symptoms such as these cover much hostility, often unconscious, and in their extreme passivity are immensely vengeful and aggressive. Treatment has a low success rate. Friedman's doctors found that they often needed to confront the patients with their underlying hostility. One doctor, driven to desperation by a patient, found herself saying, 'You seem to be a very strong woman and you have managed to reduce your husband to impotence. If you are so strong, perhaps you can restore him.' It was apparently reassuring to this woman to have her aggression recognized so straightforwardly, because the couple was then able to have intercourse.

Less severe symptoms also contain the seeds of revenge, a need to control, a fixation on one or other parent or lack of confidence in gender identity. There may be no severe problem in bed if the underlying preoccupation, doubt, aggression or impulse is contained and given room for expression in other areas of life outside the bedroom. For example, some jobs or hobbies allow verbally or physically for sublimation of impulses. Hard physical jobs conducted in a same-sex group can support and strengthen a weak sense of gender identity. When retirement or redundancy occurs, a sexual problem may manifest itself. The impulse previously contained or harnessed in the work setting becomes dangerous and inhibiting in bed when there is no alternative outlet.

Jack Kettlewell became impotent within fourteen days of having left the prison service. It was never fully explained why he had to leave, but we can imagine that the ardour with which he had previously performed his duties (always the first to take on extra work) had gone too far. Two years later, when he obtained work as a bailiff executing writs, he regained his potency. Stuart Carter had been a caring and loving father while exercising consider-able skill in a steelworks. When he was made redundant and no longer had this outlet for the expression of his masculinity, he became less confident in the caring aspects of his personality, almost as if afraid he would become all woman. He and his wife decided not to put off having the second child they had planned, despite the financial uncertainty. Conception was external proof of masculinity. Unlike Jack Kettlewell, his sexual desire increased when he was out of work and his wife had difficulty in keeping up with his need.

Some people have grounds for fearing the consequences of their hetero-sexuality. It is not uncommon for a couple who have had the sadness of producing a heavily disabled or diseased baby to find that they later lose their desire for intercourse. At a rational level, and fully conversant with con-traceptive methods, they know their fear is unwarranted. But if actual proof of unfortunate outcome confirms an underlying fear, which previously they may have repressed well, unconscious panic wins over rational argument. William Hyatt had been told too often as a child that 'the sins of the fathers' shall be visited on the 'third and fourth generation of them that hate Him'. As a young man he stoutly said 'nonsense' to himself. Only when his third child was born severely handicapped did his potency fail. It is generally true that people are in the greatest difficulties when the external world confirms their worst fears about themselves, and are at their happiest when it confirms their best fantasies.

The combination of early fantasy and external fact is what leaves many people in severe difficulty after being sexually abused as children. Seductive behaviour on the part of a child is natural. The child needs to know that he can win the heart of his parents, but also that such feelings can be handled safely. When the parent is consciously or unconsciously seductive, and the child's early fantasies are not mediated and finally renounced, the young person can remain fixated in love like the Brünnhildes and Queen Bees mentioned earlier in this chapter. However distasteful and frightening an act of incest may have been, the earlier fantasies of wanting the parent for the self may leave a trail of connected guilt.

Today there is much public concern about the amount of incest that occurs and is now coming to light. It is unfortunate that when a problem of this sort gets so much publicity it can become the bandwagon on which those who desperately want attention jump. Phone-in services can be bedevilled by hoax calls. As therapists, we have over the years become suspicious of the adult patient who too openly and easily confesses inces-tuous experience, putting this as the first and foremost cause of all their problems. When incest is the genuine major cause of sexual and relationship problems, it usually emerges only slowly, and there is considerable con-fusion over guilt, fantasies and what actually happened. When, as it were, it is flaunted as *The Problem*, it is more often being used as a defence against a deeper, underlying one.

We repeat again that many sexual problems are the direct heritage of infancy and, in that respect, are not easily overcome. For many people, some sexual failure, temporary or otherwise, is made worse by the immense current cultural emphasis on passionate sex being the 'be all and end all', with the implication of failure if they are not easily roused to orgasm regardless of what else is going on in their lives. June and Robert Braithwaite achieved much better intercourse both in and out of bed when she learned to understand and value his greater need of physical sensation and he became less worried by her being different and placing a lower value on physical experience. She felt much less used and abused when she could distinguish whether his hugs were genuine offers of warmth and love towards her or whether they were his means of asking for something just for himself. Derek and Elsie Young did not overcome their sexual problem; excitement and lack of control remained too frightening for them both. But they did learn to be less worried about it, and to accept themselves for what they were, with their mutual hang-ups, weaknesses and strengths.

6. Shocks to the System: Predictable Events

RHYTHMS OF LIFE

Behind the diversity of living arrangements which go to make up individual marriages are common themes and dilemmas. There is the push for change and the pull of security, the longing for intimacy and the fear of being engulfed, the wish to be the same as others and the drive to be different. As we have said, couples are engaged in a kind of dance, moving towards each other and then drawing apart, constantly searching for a comfortable balance in their relationship. Frequently the balance is no sooner found than upset again. The most satisfying marriages are those where partners can rely upon each other both to support and to counterbalance their movements. A capacity to adapt and be flexible is a definite asset.

Every marriage is affected by events which occur outside the partnership. In the next chapter we consider events which are unexpected and which shock the couple into making a response; for example, the discovery of an affair can destabilize a relationship to the point of breakdown, although more frequently it triggers a re-evaluation of the partnership and some heart-searching as to why it was necessary to draw attention to problems in the marriage in this way. Other events, like the birth of a first child, are predictable and consciously desired. Yet in the excitement of becoming a parent it is easy to forget that for some the impact can be not so dissimilar from that caused by the discovery of a rival lover. In this chapter we shall be considering some of these 'natural' shocks to the system of marriage and asking why they upset some people and are the making of others.

By focusing on some of the difficulties people may encounter we do not wish to suggest that life is nothing but problems, nor to imply that these problems cannot be overcome. Our intention is to identify some of the pressure points in married life and indicate why they have a different impact.

While it is unwise to lay claim to there being a natural history of marriage when there are so many individual variations, there is a discernible ebb and flow in the tide of a couple's life together which forms a pattern. There is a process of two individuals joining together to form a new life, often personified by children. Some relationships have to be let go in order that new ones can flourish. As time passes this new life will change and itself be superseded, requiring a re-ordering of the couple's partnership and re-formings in the family group. This process is repeated over and over again in relation to major and minor events throughout the family life-cycle.

For a marriage to be successful, partners need to be able to handle change constructively. They need to be alive to the balance between their own needs for intimacy and independence as well as those of their partner. Moreover, account has to be taken of the needs of other generations – of children and grandparents – which impinge upon their own. All these change over time.

Change, however welcome, is usually associated with some degree of stress. Leaving home, getting married, going on holiday, promotion at work, starting a family, all require certain familiar routines and rhythms to be given up in order to make the most of a new situation. Relationships change. People seen in a different context are treated in a different way. As a result they begin to see themselves differently. New challenges summon up fresh resources, or expose areas in which resources are lacking. Assumptions may be challenged and identities affected. But the same events can affect people very differently.

Some have argued that change has a cumulative effect. Several minor changes occurring in a short space of time can have a totting-up effect, challenging and even overloading the resources people have at their disposal. Social scientists have devised a check-list of stressful events, weighted according to how serious they are. At one end of the scale the death of a spouse rates 100 points. At the other, a minor violation of the law rates 11 points. Getting married scores 50 points, a marital separation 65. The originators[1] of this stress-rating scale estimate that people who score 150 points have a 50 per cent likelihood, and those who score 300 have a 90 per cent likelihood, of developing a stress-related illness.

But this is not the full story. Factors other than events come into play to determine the impact of change. It is one thing to face a situation alone, quite another to be able to share a burden or the excitement. Family, friends and colleagues at work can provide a buffer against some of the stressful effects of change. More formally, the social procedures which initiate people into new roles and responsibilities can help to equip them to respond positively to the challenge of the new. Christenings, weddings and funerals are the rites most commonly marking the big events in life. They provide rituals which publicly mark a change of state and assemble a network of people who can offer practical and emotional support to those undergoing the change. The accessibility and helpfulness of formal services (such as health care, financial assistance and housing advice) also make a difference.

Every bit as important as the events we experience in life and the support available to us is the personal meaning of change. Within marriage the same events are continually being interpreted in different ways. A small event like mother-in-law coming to stay can have a differential impact on newly-marrieds. The mother's offer to cook the lunch may be a reassuring sign of the familiar to her son who may not long have departed from the parental home. To his wife, mother-in-law's offer can mean a devastating indictment of her cooking abilities, or, worse, a demonstration of a prior claim on her husband. If she comes from a family where she felt undermined by her own mother the effect upon her is compounded. With luck, an ensuing argument will highlight how the situation has been read differently by each partner and result in the couple being more married than before, feeling more together in themselves and with each other.

All of us look out on life through personal windows which have been shaped by past experiences. To varying degrees we all suffer from restricted vision. We are inclined to look for certain features in the landscape and ignore others. Moreover, we are conservative beings. We want our outlook to be confirmed as the right one. If events contradict the way we see things, we may either turn a blind eye or resist hotly. To see things differently means changing ourselves in some way, and most of us are reluctant to do this. We tend not to change unless we have to.

The imperative to change comes from one of two sources, each of which has positive and negative aspects. Our personal aspirations or dissatisfactions may lead us to seek out new opportunities. Alternatively they may close us in on ourselves. When we defend ourselves too rigidly against threatening aspects of change we can precipitate the very situations we seek to avert. If the fear of being alone causes us to cling ever more insistently to others we are, at some point, likely to be left more on our own than we would otherwise be. Here an inner momentum brings us face to face with ourselves and we can choose between perpetuating the old pattern or learning from our experience. Alternatively, an external event like the death of a loved one can precipitate change. Then we simply cannot carry on our lives as if nothing has happened. The event can, of course, be a happy one and create openings which allow us to 'break the mould' of earlier restrictions. Through events of different kinds we are likely to be put in touch with aspects of ourselves which previously have been overlooked – we are given a jolt, and have to make a bridge between how things used to be and how they have become. Without that bridge the continuity of meaning in our lives is threatened.[2] Some way has to be found of bringing past and present into line.

Every transition needs to involve a mourning process. Although it is most obvious and acute when there is an actual death (and we go on to describe reactions to the death of a partner in the next chapter), some mourning is appropriate to the many minor deaths which occur in the course of married life. Any change involves a mixture of gain and loss, loss and gain. As well as celebrating the new, people must let go of that part of their past which is now redundant. The prospective gains cannot be fully harnessed and enjoyed if the losses are not first acknowledged and then mourned. The process of mourning, so clearly mapped out in bereavement studies, applies also to getting married, starting a family, letting children go, retiring, and to a myriad other changes which affect marriage. The intensity of reaction is normally very much less in these cases than after a severe loss such as bereavement but, even so, people can be surprised by their lethargy, sadness, even depression and bursts of irritation, which disturb what was expected to be so happy. After any major change it is important to give oneself some moratorium – suspend some activities – to allow feelings concerned with the loss of the old to be lived through. The conservative self needs time to catch up. And, if it is at all possible, the number of changes which could occur at any one time is better curtailed and staggered.

Inevitable changes in married life provide jolts which can stimulate growth and development. Through them we can come to know ourselves and others a little better.

FROM TWO TO THREE

In Chapter 4 we described the transition into marriage, that process of disengagement from family, friends and the single state of mind that is necessary to enable a lifelong commitment to be made to another person. We examined the public and private covenants which underwrite this commitment, and the purpose they serve in enabling people to develop both within themselves and in their relationships with others. In this chapter we outline some of the transitions which normally take place in the course of married life and the challenges they pose.

One of the most significant changes in marriage occurs with the transition to parenthood. In the short term, becoming a parent is a stressful business. That is not to deny the pleasures that children bring. Nor is it to imply that difficulties cannot be resolved. Normally they can and will. Because the experience of parenthood is to some extent idealized in our culture we have chosen to draw attention to stressful aspects of the transitions involved. The pleasures of being a parent speak for themselves. Leaving aside the reactions of friends and relatives to changes in their roles and relationships (and the generational shift involved in becoming a grandparent has its ups and downs) the transition from wife to mother, and from husband to father, is also a transition from two to three. In this change, it is often the woman who is the more vulnerable half of the marital partnership.

DEPRESSED MOTHERS

The phenomenon of 'post-natal depression' is perhaps the best chronicled negative condition associated with becoming a mother. This blanket term covers the 'blues' at one end of the spectrum (affecting between 70 and 80 per cent of all women in the first week or so after birth) to the post-puerperal psychosis which temporarily hospitalizes three in every thousand mothers. Between these extremes comes the chronic depression found to have affected one in three mothers with pre-school age children in a London study of working-class families.[3]

Explanations for these conditions vary according to the type of depression under examination and who is doing the categorizing. For example, medical explanations of the 'blues' tend to favour as the principal causative element biochemical changes taking place in a woman's body during pregnancy and immediately after birth. Sociological explanations of the same condition draw attention to the hospital environment in which mothers have their babies, and to the debilitating effects of medical procedures and technology during labour and delivery.

Some emphasize the idealization of motherhood as a social phenomenon, arguing that the all-sacrificing, good-mother image is the cultural stereotype of feminity. Women then feel a choice has to be made – one that has been socially determined – between attempting to conform or relinquishing their claim to a 'proper' sexual identity. From this perspective, the remedy lies not so much in providing personal help as in attempting to reconcile the activities of women and the values of society more effectively.[4]

Most people would agree that parenthood is not of itself a sufficient explanation for the severe stress symptoms and degree of depression among young mothers. The experience of becoming a mother has to be understood in a personal and social context which takes account of predisposing factors such as poor housing, an unsupportive marriage, lack of employment and financial difficulties. The diversity of circumstances and meanings, both social and personal, will then interact with each other, explaining why some will cheerfully survive the worst material hardships while others, who may be well-provided for in terms of physical resources, fall at the first fence.

In the longer term, a woman's feeling about herself as a mother will affect her moods and how she behaves in that role. Her relationship with her own mother will be a very important determining factor. A firm identification allows daughters to take inside themselves the resources of their mothers so that when their time comes they, too, are equipped as parents. If the relationship between mother and daughter is poor, a good relationship may be 'invented' to compensate for the shortcomings of that relationship. In later life the daughter may find herself self-condemned as, without adequate inner resources, she fails to live up to the ideal standards she has set for herself. In this situation the psychological process known as 'splitting', which we have described earlier, is apt to occur. To recap, idealized 'good' relationships (often the product of fantasy) are unconsciously separated from the 'bad' relationships in which failure, anger, depression and other negatively connoted feelings are experienced. All that is 'good' may then be retained for the conscious self while the 'bad' is unconsciously attributed to others. Conversely, the sense of failure may be retained while others are perceived to hold the key to all success. A third variant is that the 'good' and 'bad' qualities are apportioned to different people outside, in much the same way as children believe in and distinguish between fairies and witches, cowboys and Indians, empires of good and evil.

Liddie Heath became very depressed after the birth of her first child, a baby boy. She had attended all the preparation classes available during pregnancy and had looked forward to giving birth naturally and effortlessly. In the event there had been complications during labour and the baby was born by caesarean section while she was under general anaesthetic. When Liddie returned home she had difficulties breastfeeding her baby and quickly gave up in favour of using a bottle. She felt tired and exhausted and lost confidence in herself. Despite receiving a lot of help she gave up looking after the child, asking her mother-in-law to do so with increasing frequency. But the more help she received in looking after her son, the more depressed and critical of others she became.

Many women complain of feeling chronically tired, tied to the home, unattractive, disinterested in sex and generally overwhelmed during early parenthood. Most respond well to offers of practical and emotional help. But Liddie had difficulty using help. Despite describing a happy childhood, she told her therapist about how she had been brought up in a family where she felt unappreciated and undervalued. Both her parents had careers, and Liddie felt under a constant pressure from inside herself to prove herself to them. She had not got on well with her mother who, she felt, had either left her alone or taken her over completely. Liddie had trained and practised as an accountant before she started a family, but she had not really enjoyed her work. Having a baby was going to change all that. She would be the perfect mother whom others would notice and admire.

The realities of parenthood for her were, as for most people, different from what she expected. She felt angry with others for robbing her of her ideal fantasy of motherhood. The doctors had let her down, her baby was difficult, her mother-in-law was not good enough. Her own sense of failure was projected into others in order to ward off a depression about herself which finally overwhelmed her and was not to lift for some years. She invited help and then behaved towards those who helped as if they were incompetent or, like her mother, were taking over. She even began to resent the attention her baby boy received from others, as if he had displaced her. An actual baby had awakened the baby inside herself; she wanted less to be a mother than to have a baby, so that by feeding him she could in some way nourish herself. This identification between mother and baby is a normal part of parenthood. In Liddie's case, however, it had brought her face to face with a disenchanted childhood which she had not wanted to recognize.

DISPOSSESSED FATHERS

Men are subject to two contradictory pressures when they become fathers. On the one hand there is a strong (and sometimes unconscious) pull to identify with the mother and to share – even take over – her role.

During pregnancy and the months immediately following birth, men frequently identify at an unconscious level with their partners. It is quite common to find them taking an unusual interest in pets, putting on weight, complaining of backache and toothache, or being faddy about food – behaviour more usually associated with pregnant women. This process is aided and abetted by the trend over the past twenty years to encourage the active participation of fathers in the process of childbirth itself. The Duke of Edinburgh saw none of his children being born, but no one was surprised at Prince Charles' presence at the birth of Prince William. Once the baby is born, bouts of anger, sulking and withdrawing in the early stages of parenthood suggest that the identification continues; men can sometimes be as post-natally depressed as their partners.

On the other hand there are pressures to divide. Economic and social realities, together with the legacy of traditional parental practice, limit the opportunities for men to become actively involved as parents.

The ideological commitment to equality between the sexes reinforces expectations about male participation in the very early stages of parenthood which may subsequently be disappointed by social, biological and practical realities. The elation of witnessing birth may be followed by a sense of disorientation at being a displaced person. Men cannot breastfeed babies, nor can they experience what it is like to have carried a child, however much their partners may have encouraged them to feel the moving infant inside the belly. The closeness of pregnancy is frequently followed by a sense of separateness once the baby is born. Outside the family, the claims of work and career (which may be at their strongest at this time) may either frustrate paternal longings or provide compensation for the displacement. Yet times are changing. Brian Jackson[5] wrote eloquently about the still frequently thwarted aspirations of young fathers today to be different from the invisible or authoritarian men they remember their own fathers as having been. For some fathers, the motivation to be involved with their children has powerful psychological roots.

Liddie Heath's husband, Richard, was the model of a helpful partner when their son was born. He had been with Liddie through the various pre-natal classes, lying on the floor with her and learning the breathing exercises. Back at home with their baby he was quick to be the one to change the nappies and administer the bottle feed once Liddie had given up breastfeeding. Behind his conscious wish to help was an unconscious fear of losing his wife to the baby. His own mother had been, and to some extent remained, an intrusive presence in his life, and he had started to shut her out by keeping busy and doing everything for himself. He dealt with his fear of being controlled by, in some sense, becoming like his mother, and he tried to earn the unconditional attention of others. When he became a father, he unwittingly undermined and displaced his wife in order not to be undermined and displaced himself. These factors continued to make it more difficult for him to provide the separateness and space that Liddie needed if she were to develop her limited confidence in herself as a mother. In consequence he became, in Liddie's eyes, the kind of mother her own mother had been – one who disabled her by taking over.

THE CHANGING COUPLE

As well as celebrating, some measure of depression is an appropriate response for both men and women when they become parents. There are losses involved. Motherhood today often involves giving up paid employment (although nowadays for shorter periods than in the past), and with it the sense of identity and community that work affords. Thirty years ago this change would have been more likely to coincide with marriage; today it coincides with becoming a parent, and its significance may be underrated as maternity leave holds open the option of a very early return to work. The birth of a baby results in some loss of intimacy in marriage, a loss of space at home, a loss of time to oneself, and a loss of physical and financial resources to manage additional demands and responsibilities. There may also be losses in terms of the hopes, expectations and images of parenthood which have not been borne out by experience. There is also a loss for those who have valued shared activities and similarity. Children separate parents and define their roles along traditional gender lines. There is a process of segregation which can rebound on the marriage.

With the arrival of a child a woman tends to see herself as parent first and partner second. This can be expressed very physically in the way breasts are now regarded as being for feeding babies rather than for making love, and most couples experience tensions over their sexual relationship in the early months and even years of parenthood. They have to become used to the parent in themselves and in their partner, as well as to the baby. Men tend to put greater store by their work once there are children (perhaps because of the burden of being the sole earner, and perhaps because their place at work is not unchallenged in the way it may be at home) and housework, which before may have been shared equally, often now falls to the woman. This can be a major source of conflict. Six months after the first birth, a wife's evaluation of marriage is likely to be lower than that of her husband, and by eighteen months conflict may reach a peak. The significance of these changes is that the partners, having come together to make children, are now having to move apart again and manage differences which parenthood has made unavoidable.

When roles become more segregated, as they do after the birth of a baby, even when both parents continue to go out to work, people are less able to avoid their envy of the opposite sex and of the baby who receives so much care and attention. They may or may not be conscious of their envy, but it will affect their marriage. In terms of the unconscious choice of partner, and the unconscious covenant between partners which we described in Chapters 3 and 4, it is likely that extreme envy marries the envy in the other, and the defence of splitting may well be used by the couple. For example, the wife and mother has the opportunity to soothe her own unconscious envy of the baby vicariously by the devoted care she gives to him. The husband, feeling deprived of the care he previously had from his wife, and sometimes carrying her projected envy, is left even more envious than he otherwise would be. One of the fantasies of the envious is that the other has everything. This leaves the person feeling empty – sometimes totally empty. Husbands may put even more effort and hours into employment outside the home to fill the void.

Wives, increasingly tired from the non-stop demands of a baby whose cries they cannot resist (sometimes because of their own vicarious need, not necessarily the baby's), then feel even more abandoned. The constant repression of their own envy can add to the burden of tiredness. (Over-deployed defences are exhausting.) Fantasies of the joys and excitement of working life abound in the mind. For men, it can seem as if the reverse is true. Both partners find it difficult to hear the other and appreciate the needs of the other. She cannot hear that much of his business life is tedious, worrying, tiring and not all that exciting; he cannot hear and see her boredom and exhaustion in his fantasy that she is the one who has everything – not having to earn, not having to stir out each morning and so comfortable with *only* a baby to look after. When both work, similar feelings may be attached to other wives.

Envy of the other sex and envy of babies go hand in hand. One may get displaced on to the other, or one, a problem in its own right, may be used as a defence against the other. In its most extreme form envy underlies much marital violence and baby battering, the actual batterer often carrying not only his own unconscious envy but that of his partner as well. But, as we have suggested earlier, few of us are totally free of envy, or conscious of all the different facets of our envy. Nor do we easily associate ourselves with violent behaviour. We suggest, however, that the tiredness experienced by young couples in the first months of a baby's life is not just the result of broken nights, change of role, anxiety as to the well-being of so small and vulnerable a being, and doubts about being a good enough parent, but is also related to the strain of exercising a defence against envy of the baby to whom so much care and comfort is offered. It is hardly decent to envy the baby to whom so much is owed.

The more couples are able to tolerate differences in their partnership – between men and women, and between babies and parents – the less will the satisfactions of being a parent and being a married partner be eroded by children. Past experiences affect how comfortable people are with differences and disparities in their marriage. Having to be more separate can, for some people, resurrect memories of earlier separations which were particularly painful for them. Illness, displacement by a younger brother or sister, or the divorce of parents are experiences from the past which can be interwoven with a current separation, overdetermining the strength of feelings and reactions in the present day. Quite unconsciously, children may be regarded as rivals for a partner's attention, or, when they cry inconsolably, critics of a mother's competence. Real children stir to life the child that lives on in every parent.[6]

Yet children also bring immense rewards and satisfaction. A chance is given to recover past joys and heal old wounds as well as to provide the experiences which children will, in their turn, look back upon with love and affection. Although, for some, the tragedies of one generation will be repeated in the next, people can and do learn from experience.

THE MIDDLE YEARS

For most people, the middle years of marriage are the child-rearing years; life revolves around running the 'family business'. These are the years when the satisfactions from marriage are likely to dip. There is remarkable consensus among family researchers showing a 'U' shaped association between levels of marital satisfaction and the child-rearing years. Satisfaction drops to its lowest point when children are still at home waiting to start school. There may be some recovery when they go to school, but the dip will reassert itself during the teenage years. As children leave home marital satisfaction tends to pick up again.

General pictures of what happens during the middle years are inevitably flawed, but they suggest that a change often takes place in marriage at that time and that for many people satisfactions come from sources outside the couple's relationship. The variety of routes taken by couples make it impossible to track the course most frequently taken. But if one issue is to be singled out as representing a point of potential conflict between partners at this time it will most likely concern the relationship between home and employment.[7] Role conflicts within individual marriages are taking place in a context of rapid social change and all the uncertainties that attend it. The days have passed in which Tennyson could confidently assert:

> *Man for the field and woman for the hearth:*
> *Man for the sword and for the needle she:*
> *Man with the head and woman with the heart:*
> *Man to command and woman to obey;*
> *All else confusion.*
>
> *(The Princess,* V, 427–31)

The last thirty years in Britain have seen a significant cultural change in respect of women working. Between 1973 and 1985 the proportion of women working outside the home rose from 56 to 63 per cent and the trend has continued upwards since then. Many have taken part-time jobs in service industries in order to earn money while caring for their children. In 1985 27 per cent of all wives were working in full-time employment. This proportion has been affected by falling numbers of full-time jobs, but the trend towards women working – and in areas traditionally seen as male preserves – is supported by public opinion, except when there are very young children at home. The need to work is often financial, two incomes being required to maintain heavy mortgages and what Ivan Illich, a critic of the Establishment, has called, 'the modern addiction to paralysing affluence'. (Although it was as long ago as 1884 that Marx wrote of the shift from worker as producer to worker as consumer, the degree of expendability of goods and their constant replacement by better and newer models have markedly increased during the latter half of this century.)

But the need of many women to work is personal and social as well as financial. As we mentioned in Chapter 3, the new Age of Psychology promotes and emphasizes the development and self-fulfilment of the individual. During the early child-rearing years, women often need to exercise their mothering and loving capacities to the excluson of other parts of themselves. After a few years they may find that not enough of their nature is being fulfilled. They ask for more stimulus than their children provide and for the opportunity to give expression to their other creative and intellectual drives. Sometimes this can be managed by buying in domestic services. Sometimes it can occasion immense conflict within the wife between needs of self and needs of partner and children. Sometimes it triggers a fight between partners.

To be in paid employment is to be valued. Although the Victorian values embedded in Tennyson's lines continue to hold sway in many quarters, most people recognize the inequalities and injustices that result from home and work activities being allotted according to gender. Money is power, and for this reason employment continues to call the tune. If the husband has to move to another area to find work, wife and children are likely to follow (unless the price of property makes the cost of the family living together prohibitive). If she also works they must decide whose job has priority. Whereas it used to be assumed that she would follow him around the country and around the world, it is now not uncommon for wives to decide to stay put in order to further their own careers, or so that they do not disrupt their childrens' education.

Sometimes, both partners make a commitment to employment way above their commitment to family life. Home becomes little more than a dormitory, an evening and weekend extension to the office. Although the partners may remain dependent on their marriage and committed to the arrangement either for provision of a little-used but resplendent home, or for earnings to support the acquired life style, little may be shared between them socially and emotionally. In these marriages, work becomes what has been called an 'acceptable mistress'. But just as women now demand for themselves greater freedom to express different facets of the self, so too do some men, although not nearly so many of them. Some now want to be less dominated by the world of employment and demands of career. Like their wives, they want to express more of themselves and get in touch with the caring and home-making aspects of their personalities. Some have become prepared to forgo promotion if it means too much disruption of home and family and if they personally do not want the commuting life. Some, of course, have leisure time imposed on them. The number of men not working and not seeking a job has risen by a half since 1971. The employment situation has led to early retirement becoming common practice, while some younger men have come to believe they are unemployable.

These changes have profound implications for marriage. Work is a means of regulating the distance in a partnership. Too much work and people lose touch with each other; too little and they get under one another's feet. Oil-rig workers, export salesmen and servicemen have to manage part-time marriages, and so do their wives. A family which has organized itself to run smoothly in the absence of one member must repeatedly adapt to incorporate the absent member when he or she returns home. Businessmen working away from home frequently describe the tension on their return when their partners, who have been shut in with the children all week, suggest going out for dinner. When they have been eating out all the time they have been away, and are longing for an evening at home, the suggestion does not go down well. Unemployment, or increased leisure time, poses different challenges. A structure and meaning to the day has to be found from inside rather than imposed from outside.

In relation to these changes, which can evoke highly charged feelings, men and women need to continue to negotiate an acceptable balance in their relationship between being together and being apart. They need to struggle with the thorny issue of whose interests come first, and they must be ready to let go of some aspirations and commitments if they are to enjoy what they decide to do.

THREE INTO TWO

LOSING CHILDREN

The departure of children returns the parental couple to a twosome. In this new phase, many couples reap the rewards of all their efforts of the preceding years. For others, there is a grain of truth in Oscar Wilde's sardonic comment that 'in married life three is company and two none'. For children, like work, regulate distance in a marriage and provide parents with a role and sense of personal worth. After the hectic middle years, couples may renew or begin activities together for which there had not previously been time. Or partners may look at each other across the breakfast table once the children have left home and ask themselves what they still have in common.

For a longer period than in years gone by they can expect to be on their own together. Although outwardly this period resembles the beginnings of married life, it is very different. Because children now arrive later in marriage, parents may be in their fifties before the last child leaves home.

They are likely to be beset with other major changes associated with the second half of life. The menopause, career disappointments, the death of their own parents, and retirement looming on the horizon herald other separations and endings. The compensation of greater freedom may hold fewer attractions when energy is diminished. A man may be looking forward to regaining the undivided attention of his wife. But she may remain preoccupied with her lost children, or anxious to take advantage of her new-found independence, free of demands, including those of her husband.

Although both parents will be affected by the departure of children, the impact is likely to be most keenly felt by the woman. She is the one who will have devoted the greater part of her married life to the job of child-raising and who will have invested a large part of herself in the children. Even a career woman will have organized her life and work to take account of the children in a way men, at present, rarely have to do. So it is the woman who will experience the first withdrawal symptoms. Some will revel in having more time for themselves; others will feel lost. There is evidence to suggest that withdrawal symptoms include heightened irritability, a tendency to drink too much and increased susceptibility to illness and depression. Educated women seem to be at a particular disadvantage because they are expected, and expect themselves, to accept the loss gracefully and suppress irrational feelings associated with a process which is not unlike mourning. In short, the loss of children is often the major adjustment of middle age for women, equivalent in its impact to the loss of employment for men.

The crux of the experience is where the couple's source of self-esteem lies: this is crucial to how the powerful parent–child attachments are managed. The degree of ease with which sexuality was handled by the couple's parents will be reflected in the way they handle the sexuality of their own children. They may put pressure on their children to leave and live the life they missed out on. Or, if they had difficulty leaving home when they were young, they may unconsciously place obstacles in the way of their own children doing so when the time comes. How was marriage affected by parenthood at the very beginning? How did they manage separation when the children were very young? What was it like at home when the youngest child started school? What are their feelings about dating? Is there enough going for the partners – both as a couple and as individuals – to allow them to relinquish their role as parents? Will they feel empty on the last child's departure and give substance to what is often called the 'empty nest' syndrome of marriage? A satisfying marriage to which parents are happy to devote time eases the loss. Letting go is more difficult when children have become comforting substitutes for disappointment in a marriage.

Inevitably, the process is affected by fantasies which surround leaving home. Pauline Crook had difficulty separating from an intense attachment to her own mother, whose death, shortly after Pauline's marriage, aroused her guilt. She conceived and gave birth to her only child and transferred this intensity of attachment to her daughter, Chloe. During the child-rearing years her husband, Dan, was relegated to the sidelines. Having himself come from a close family he did not at first regard his wife's involvement with Chloe as unusual. When the time came for Chloe to leave home, Pauline became unduly worried about her health and constantly clucked over her like a mother hen to make sure she was alright. Only at this point did Dan protest about being neglected. The relationship between Pauline and Chloe then became a major source of conflict in the marriage. In relation to Chloe, Pauline and Dan lived out the conflicts of their own adolescence. Their situation was similar to the well-known triangular struggle between the Barretts of Wimpole Street, Elizabeth colluding with her father in an illness which kept her tied to home until Robert Browning won her away from invalidism to health through marriage.

The challenge for couples when children leave home is to adapt their intimate relationship, relinquishing some aspects of parenthood to become partners once more, and to develop new sources of satisfaction and meaning in life. For some parents, perhaps the over-committed ones, the hope of early grandparenthood may allow the parental knot to be slackened, if not untied. For others, the turn of the generations will have a more ominous feel. But for most the change will ring in new pleasures.

The conscious wish of every parent is to launch their children as competent, independent adults, and much satisfaction and pride is to be gained from this process. But in this very satisfaction lies the difficulty that for twenty years or more a good deal of self-esteem and affirmation has depended upon the parenting role. As it is relinquished, and this source of daily confirmation dries up, there may well spring up doubts about self-worth and purpose. The temptation to hang on to the past can then be strong. It may be supported by the behaviour of a child sensitive to the parent's feelings. But the stunting of development in this way is likely to result in parental guilt and some spoiling of the achievements parents and children have accomplished together earlier on.

There are many different ways of making the break. When parents and children have been passionately attached to each other it may be that the only way to leave is to have a blow-up. The stag-fight between fathers and sons, for example, which allows children to leave home abruptly and in high dudgeon may, having achieved what was dreaded, prepare the ground for loving relationships to be restored on a new basis. It sounds as if this was Mark Twain's experience:

> When I was a boy of fourteen, my father was so ignorant I could hardly stand the old man around. But when I got to be twenty-one, I was astonished at how much he had learned in seven years.

The position of the child in the family may affect the separating process. Older children may have greater ease in leaving because of the hostage children left behind; indeed, the last child may have been conceived, as many late children are, to postpone the final loss. On the other hand, if the parents and older children can manage the transition successfully, the way out for the youngest may be eased. The departure of a 'special' child may be particularly problematic because he or she may have invoked part of the parents' own history, or because the child performed a vital role in the family such as 'go-between' or communicator. Children who have to leave a lone parent, whether single from death or divorce, are obviously going to be more troubled and guilty about the possible loneliness and vulnerability of the one they leave behind than children who know there are others to carry that burden. If a child has stepped into an absent parent's shoes another dimension of loss and anxiety is added to the transition. Similarly, an only child may have a tough time leaving home without the support of brothers and sisters. And the process is not just one way. Children miss their parents. An elderly lady admitted crying every night for the first three weeks of her marriage because she missed her sister and widowed mother so much.

Alongside anxiety about loss must be placed a parallel feeling best expressed by the indignant snort of a parent of four 'children' in their twenties: 'Empty nest? What empty nest? I'd like to know when it will be empty!' And this feeling is echoed by many parents whose children have successfully left home but return to visit: 'It's lovely to see them come, but it's lovely to see them go.' What about those who cannot go? When children are unable to find work they may have no option but to stay at home. What do parents do then? It is not unknown for the senior generation to move away, even go abroad, in order to tip the younger generation out of the nest.

Frequently the transition is managed with a back and forth movement, a re-meeting and re-parting by which the slow process of building separate lives is accomplished. When an added stress threatens a newly won independence there may need to be a temporary reuniting. Even if parents succeed in coming to terms with letting their children go, their best efforts are likely to be undermined by the 'dirty washing' gambit, or proprietorial claims to 'my room' which the child will not relinquish. For the rule is that while children may always blame parents for their problems, this privilege is not allowed to work in reverse.

LOSING WORK

If children are the third parties women have to relinquish to become part of a twosome again, work – 'the acceptable mistress' – is the equivalent for men. Retirement is for men what the children leaving home is for women. A new structure to the day and a new meaning in life have to be worked out. Not least, a new balance must be established in the marriage when people have more time to be together. As at the beginning of marriage, the right distance must be established if a satisfying new type of pairing is to work.

For some, freedom from the 'old toad' of work may constitute sheer delight. They may feel entitled to indulge in what previously would have felt irresponsible. Meaningful activity may develop from a variety of interests and be enjoyed with much more breathing space. If they can tolerate the uncertainty of not knowing how this last period of their lives will develop, they may well be surprised by what 'takes off'.

If they are frightened of the prospective freedom and plan their retirement too tightly, they may find their life becomes as structured as when they were working. Husbands who cannot bear a slowing-down and are unable to find new meaningful activities may start taking on some of the jobs around the house formerly done by their wives. This may not be an altogether welcome development for the wives and they may react strongly to their territory being invaded in this way. If they do not protest they may experience the feelings of redundancy which properly belong to their husbands. The husband's defence against the discomfort of losing an important source of meaning in life is secured at his wife's expense, and, in the long term, of course, at his own. There are many elderly marriages in which one partner has been debilitated, even made ill, to protect the other from feeling useless.

Arthur and Joan Peabody had been married forty-two years when Arthur retired from work. Joan had made running the home her life's work, and she devoted herself to looking after Arthur. He was content with this arrangement while he could channel his inclination to worry into the problems he faced at work. When he retired, he began to worry about Joan. After a small embolism was discovered on her leg, Arthur insisted on looking after her, sitting her in a chair day after day and taking over the jobs in the home that she used to do. He had felt off colour and low in spirits when he retired from work, and he talked about how much he had come back to life once Joan needed his care. Joan, on the other hand, felt iller and more depressed because of what had happened. She was angry with Arthur for taking over her life, but she did not allow herself to know it. So she settled into doing less and less, becoming more overtly aggressive in her demands. Only when Arthur went down with shingles was she able to come back to life.

One very big difference between the early years of marriage and those after retirement is that with retirement what was the future of the couple has become their past. Retirement marks the beginning of the final phase of life, and it is only a short step from there to begin thinking about the end of life itself. For some people, this immense thought helps them to savour what time is left to them. For others, fear of death, and the process of dying or of the final separation from their partner, can cast a deep shadow. Although, biologically speaking, the process of dying begins at birth, the first half of life is about growing, mastering the external world, begetting children, acquiring money and social position – a process which is very much orientated to the world outside. The second half of life demands that people draw on the resources they have accumulated within themselves.

One of the uncertainties for retired couples is knowing how long they will have together. How far ahead can they plan? As we noted in Chapter 1, the late stages of marriage have been extended dramatically this century. Whereas life expectancy was 48 for men and 52 for women around 1900, it is now 72 and 78 respectively. Some planning ahead is now realistic upon retirement. But in making the change, attention has to be paid to giving up a work mentality and the life-style that goes with it if couples are to be free to take on a new way of life. A healthy balance between meaningful activity and disengagement has to take into account the prospect of failing physical strength and emotional resources. Partners are having to come to terms with depending upon others when their own powers are failing. To a greater or lesser degree, life will have prepared them for the final test of growing old gracefully. Couples are challenged by the greater time they have together to invest more in marriage but in the certain knowledge that before too long one or other will be on their own again.

The natural history of marriage does not follow a defined course even when couples stay together until one partner dies. Individuals are faced with a succession of choices, each providing a combination of loss and gain, with the only certainty that at some point, in as yet unknown circumstances, there will be a parting of the ways. That is the price of commitment.

7. *Shocks to the System: Betrayal*

TRAGEDY: WHEN THE BOTTOM FALLS OUT OF YOUR LIFE

Some people, deeply pessimistic about themselves, never believing in the possibility of their own luck, can go through life always expecting the worst. The majority, imbued with a normal amount of optimism, generally expect things to go their way, believing that disaster, if it comes at all, will strike others, not them. In Chapter 4, we mentioned that many young people make their marriage vows in good faith, truly believing that their marriage will be one of those that survive, that their love will persist, that the children they want will be born healthy, grow to adulthood and outlast them. Only in old age, they think, they may be bereaved by the loss of their partner. When unpleasant and unpredictable events occur, they can be shocked to the core.

Tragedies affect people in different ways. We can often be surprised by the varying responses of our relatives, friends and acquaintances because they are so different from those we would expect of ourselves. What one person can survive emotionally can be totally traumatic for another. What is devastating to one person can be merely unfortunate to another. Although some tragedies, like the loss of a child, would be devastating to most people, it is not always what has actually happened to a person which feels so unbearable but how that person perceives what has happened to him and how this perception reverberates on his inner world. We can never fully understand the suffering of another because, as H. A. Williams has said, suffering does not take place in a vacuum, but only in relationship to a particular life history.[1] Different people have varying degrees of inner resource when they are the victims of some catastrophe. Although the reaction of most people at the time of impact would be, 'Why me?', some people mature through loss and sorrow. Others crumble and their natures appear to change for the worse; they remain bitter and fail to come to terms with the loss they have suffered and to readjust to the new circumstances of their life.

When an event concerns loss, grief is a normal reaction. Grieving is a process which goes through a number of stages. Its purpose changes over time. It begins with an attempt to protect oneself from the full implications of the loss, it continues with attempts to recover the loved person and concludes with the mourning which allows for the loss to be accepted and for life to be lived once more.

Those who have studied the experience of bereavement report the shock and disbelief which follow the news of the loss, especially one which has occurred unexpectedly. A sense of numbness, lasting anything from a few hours to days or even weeks, acts as a kind of anaesthetic against the painful realization of what has occurred. 'This isn't real, it isn't happening to me' is the kind of self-proffered reassurance given by the detached self to that other part which is in danger of feeling.

Then feelings break through. There is usually a period of restlessness, alarm and yearning, interspersed with moments of acute anxiety which can feel like fear. C. S. Lewis wrote about this in his autobiographical account, *A Grief Observed*:

> No one ever told me that grief felt so like fear. I am not afraid, but the sensation is like being afraid. The same fluttering in the stomach, the same restlessness, the yearning. I keep on swallowing. At other times it feels like being mildly drunk, or concussed.
>
> There is a sort of invisible blanket between the world and me. I find it hard to take in what anyone says. Or, perhaps, hard to want to take it in. It is so uninteresting. Yet I want the others to be about me. I dread the moments when the house is empty.

The moments of intense pining become more frequent as the experience of loss becomes unavoidable. A widow in Parke's[2] study of bereavement described her compulsion to seek out her dead husband: 'Everywhere I go I am searching for him; in crowds, in church, in the supermarket. I keep on scanning the faces. People must think I'm odd.' And sometimes this search is rewarded by apparent sightings or dreams in which the lost partner returns.

Reaching a peak a month or so after bereavement, and in ordinary circumstances occurring intermittently for about a year, are expressions of anger and protest about the loss. Although such outbursts may seem illogical to the outsider, especially one who has been trying to offer support and comfort, they can be understood as last-ditch attempts to reverse the loss. In Chapter 2 we referred to the protests of young children separated from their parents and the function of these protests in recalling those who are loved and enlisting the support of others in the search. The same unconscious logic applies in adult bereavement. Paul Scott describes the yearning and reproach of the newly widowed Mrs Smalley in *Staying On*:

> . . . but now, until the end, I shall be alone, whatever I am doing: here as I feared amid the alien corn, waking, sleeping, alone for ever and ever. I cannot bear it . . . I hold out my hand to you, Tusker, beg you to take it and take me with you. How can you make me stay here by myself while you yourself go home?

As one writer on mourning has stated, love does not fully explain grief.[3] The fundamental crisis of bereavement arises not just from loss of another, but also from loss of self. Familiar thoughts and behaviour no longer make sense. Thus, the later stages of mourning involve rebuilding identity and finding new reasons for living. Sadness and depression replace the numbness and anger characteristic of the earlier stages, as the loss is taken on board and people begin the long journey back to participating in a life which has fundamentally changed. The work of grieving will continue until this adjustment is complete, and the process often extends over a considerable period of time, involving years rather than months.

For some the work of grieving will never be completed. For others, grieving may result in a new vitality and purpose in life. It seems it is easier to recover from the loss of a deeply loving relationship than from the loss of a highly ambivalent one. The anger subsides more quickly, happy memories take hold and drive out images of a mutilated body or wasting illness. Good memories warm the heart. And there is less guilt for what was or was not said or done while there was still time. Once through the worst of the grief, experience of a satisfying, trusting and loving relationship leaves hope that it may be found and achieved again. If the relationship was stormy, uncaring, even hostile, the grief may be more intense, more prolonged and imbued with guilt.

Those who have dealt satisfactorily with loss earlier in their lives know from previous experience that it can be encompassed, grief survived and a new life made. In this knowledge they can allow themselves to grieve once more. Their minds are strong enough to carry the mixture of feelings involved in the normal grief process. Those who were bereaved or severely deprived in childhood when their minds were not strong enough to bear the disturbance of the conflicting anger and yearning will rely overmuch on defences of denying and splitting. There is much clinical evidence to show that when a major loss is not properly mourned at the time, a subsequent loss rebounds on the first, and then a double grief breaks through the defensive barriers. Double grief can be quite overwhelming, out of proportion to the later loss and unduly persistent. When, in these cases, a person seeks therapy, much of the mourning they will need to do has to concern the first as well as the later loss.

For most people the intensity of grief is related to the intensity of involvement with the lost person or object. Different levels of involvement determine whether an event, disruption or loss is tragic to one person and not necessarily so to another. Intensity of involvement is a yardstick which runs through the themes of this chapter.

LOST PARTNERS

The untimely and unpredicted death of one partner in a fully committed and lively marriage leaves a grief-stricken widow or widower. Susan Hill's book *In the Springtime of the Year* conveys most powerfully something of the intense pain of loss in a young marriage. The losses are multiple and may involve some or all of loss of love, of closest companion, of sexual pleasure, of emotional and practical support, of expected income and of previous life-style. For the most heavily involved, and those with little separate identity (for example, wives whose whole life was organized round the demands of the husband's career, sometimes even to the extent of being incorporated into the actual job like some vicars' or diplomats' wives), bereavement may feel like losing the whole purpose and meaning of life. Despite the irrationality of such emotions, it can feel like the ultimate betrayal: 'How could he desert me? How could he let me down like this?'

Earlier in this book we wrote about the choice of marriage partner and distinguished between marriages based on a fit of strong identification and those based on a fit of complementarity (recognizing, of course, every shading in between). It seems that when a marriage has been based on identification rather than complementarity, the bereaved partner has more difficulty in coming to terms with and tolerating the finality of separation than when it is based on complementarity. In younger people the grief may be very prolonged, and the intensity of the first impact of loss temporarily overwhelming.

In older people, grief may overcome. In a continuing identification, the

123

heart gives up figuratively and literally. This second death, often within a few months, sometimes within days, can surprise relatives, especially when there was no previous indication of any illness. Ethel Browning was in her late sixties when her husband, Bertrand, had a serious stroke. Well supported by their three daughters, she nursed him for two years. Physically dependent on her, he could not bear her to be out of his sight. After registering his death, she had a serious heart attack and was rushed to hospital. Two days later, when walking up the ward for the first time, she collapsed and died. Until Bertrand's illness she had been the overtly dependent partner and in middle age had had great difficulty in being separated from him when she needed to go into hospital for a fortnight. She had mustered her resources to keep him alive when he became ill, but when he died it was as if she had to follow him into death.

When the marriage has been based predominantly on complementarity, and on a reciprocal projective system, the grief may be immense and deeply disturbing, but often, after the mourning, the widowed take on a new strength. In having to take back into themselves what previously had been projected into their partner, they become fuller and better integrated, in touch with more parts of themselves than before. This can sometimes be apparent when an overtly dependent person, reliant on the resource of the partner, finds new depths of purpose and ability when widowed. It seems then as if the deceased partner achieved strength at the price of the survivor's weakness. The original covenant may have been invested with much hope of getting a better distribution of strength and weakness in each partner. When this fails in a marriage, 'the crisis of bereavement' can, as Pincus has described, 'reactivate and renew the original hope or therapeutic drive for growth and self-integration'.[4] The bereaved alone can achieve 'some aspect of what the couple could not achieve together'. This process should not be confused with the defensive one of merely aping the deceased, doing what they would have done in a constant attempt to keep them alive. This constitutes a denial of loss, rather than a coming to terms with it.

Always a problem for grief-stricken adults is how to do well by grief-stricken children. Having to continue to provide and care can give some meaning to life, which otherwise might have disappeared altogether. But how difficult to listen to *their* grief, so important because of the misconnections of facts they can often make, blaming themselves for the tragedy of the lost parent. Fantasies need to be told and heard if they are to be corrected. Children need time, attention, comfort and encouragement to share their grief, and like adults, time to grieve on their own. In their deepest grief, adults and children need to regress, curl up, escape from all demands, baby themselves or let others cosset them. In holding the children through their shock and loss, and allowing them to regress, the parent requires every ounce of adulthood. Yet time also needs to be found for the abandoned infant in the adult self, who also needs attention.

LOST BABIES

Among the thousands of women who conceive each year, some will choose to abort the foetus or will suffer the spontaneous abortion or death of an infant, just prior to, during or immediately after the birth.

Since the Abortion Act of 1967 made legal abortion in Britain much more easily available both within and outside the National Health Service, more women have been able to exercise a choice in respect of an unwanted pregnancy. Culturally, there is today a strong emphasis on rights, particularly by women in relation to childbearing issues. In 1992 there were approaching 183,000 abortions, marking a steady upward climb that has been a feature of the 1980s onwards. (This trend is attributed to the much disputed health risks associated with oral contraception.)

The majority of these abortions were outside marriage. The small percentage of people who decide on abortion within marriage may, like those outside, do so wholeheartedly but with regret, or ambivalently, with a careful weighing of pros and cons. Whether wholehearted or in conflict, they may suffer grief immediately or some time later. A study reported in 1980 contrasted the relief of some women at having got out of a difficult situation with the absence of feeling in others and with the emotional cost – grief, guilt, regret – experienced by yet others.[5] The fact that so few abortions occur within marriage (and that some people do not suffer) does not mean we should ignore possible long-term effects. As Bowlby has said, 'to argue that because 99 per cent recover, polio is a harmless infection, would obviously be absurd'.[6] Matters of life, death, destruction and loss have deep significance – both universal and particular to the individual – at different levels of consciousness. Thus people may intellectually support the reform of a stringent abortion law and at the same time be confused by their reactions when faced with what is deemed to be a personal necessity.

Few of our clients choose to speak of past abortions, because these abortions either were or are considered to have been irrelevant to the present troubles. Among the few who continue to be affected, the abortion does not have to have occurred during the marriage.

Laura Evans, who had an abortion before marriage but remained troubled about herself in a way which was affecting her marriage, eventually connected her earlier need to have an abortion with her status of having been, as she interpreted it, an unwanted child herself.

Nine months after the conception of an aborted pregnancy is a sensitive time. Jane and Michael Barnes decided to have an abortion early in their married life because Jane wanted to pursue her career and Michael did not feel ready to be a father. At the time they apparently had no difficulty in making the decision. Nine months later, sexual and interpersonal problems affected their previously satisfying relationship. When they eventually sought help, it was apparent that Jane had not made the progress in her career that she had wanted. At first she blamed circumstances. Then, on reflection, she could see how she spoilt her own chances; but it was only after her therapist had spontaneously commented, in a mixture of sadness, anger and exasperation, 'It seems that the baby died in vain,' was she then able to move forward in her career.

Mixed feelings about an abortion can, as in any shared ambivalence, be externalized and divided between the partners and become the basis of continued rows. Lawrence and Tina Green both wanted a baby but were afraid of parenting. Tina blamed Lawrence for trying to stop her having an abortion. As long as he objected, she did not have to know of her unease about abortion. As long as she opposed him he did not have to know of his fear of parenting.

In our culture, women are expected to be expressive about their feelings, men less so. When couples choose an abortion after genetic counselling, they can be seriously affected because the conception has often been planned and they have a strong wish for a normal, well baby. One study of couples who had made this choice described how some men expressed their distress either by temporarily leaving their wives or by a series of affairs.[7]

Only about 25 per cent of fathers accompany women who apply for abortions. The remaining 75 per cent receive no counselling. And they are much neglected in follow-up studies except through the subjective reports of the women. When an abortion has seriously affected a marriage and the couple have sought help, we have found that more often than not it is the husband who alludes to the event, expressing lingering regret, shame or guilt. It is the wife who then expresses surprise: 'But I never knew you felt like that.'

In the event of a spontaneous abortion, stillbirth or death within a week of birth, the loss usually comes without warning and can be quite overwhelming, shattering the hopes invested in months of planning and preparation.

It is often assumed that the less developed the foetus, the less the tragedy; similarly, that a stillbirth is less upsetting than the death of a week-old infant. This is not necessarily so. Grief for perinatal deaths is usually intense, although it may be less prolonged after miscarriage than after stillbirth or infant death. The mother of a five-month foetus can experience the same void as the mother of a newborn infant.[8] Because there is a symbiotic bond between an unborn baby and its mother, the baby being an essential part of her, its death can feel like the death of part of herself. Arms and breasts can ache to hold and nurture.

The grief after loss of a foetus, or even an embryo (defined as less than eight weeks old), carries its own particular difficulties. It may be an exceptionally lonely time for the woman. Husbands may not be able to comprehend the depth of feeling. When the baby has not been a visible and viable being, compassion from relatives, friends and medical staff may be limited. Too often and too easily, these grieving women are exhorted to find immediate comfort in the prospect of a further pregnancy on the assumption that the next one will be fruitful. However, for most women who have lost a foetus it is that infant, that part of the self, which is so much wanted.

One miscarriage increases the chance of subsequent ones, and several can result in a cycle of hope and despair, but with diminishing confidence in the ability to protect and nurture one's own creation. It is difficult to place blame elsewhere. Even after one miscarriage it is not unusual for the bereaved mother to question some of her activities – did she let herself get too tired, did she overdo this, did she make a mistake in doing that? Many women feel a failure in their own eyes and in those of parents and in-laws, who may anxiously be awaiting a grandchild.

Disposal of the body can create difficulties. How formed does the body have to be to warrant formal cremation, burial or funeral ceremony as opposed to incineration in the hospital? In the past, stillbirths have often been handled insensitively by hospital staff, parents given no choice, the little corpse whisked away for disposal as soon as possible. Now, more sensitivity is shown and bereaved parents are often encouraged to see and hold the dead baby and to say their goodbyes. Grief is helped by an image of an actual body. This provides a focus for what has been lost and starts the mourning process on its way.

Home again from hospital, husband and wife may have to face the emptiness of the newly painted nursery. In their own bedroom, they may find their sexual relationship has altered. It may become more important than during the pregnancy, being used as an expression of comfort, compensation for the loss or desire to conceive again. Or it may deteriorate because of loss of self-confidence, loss of sexual drive as a symptom of a normal grief reaction or fear of another pregnancy and its possible tragic outcome. Sometimes guilt and blame associated with the lost baby may leave people unable to allow any pleasure for themselves.

LOST CHILDREN

What if it is a child who is lost?

We pause with the enormity of the thought. It does not take much imagination to guess what it must feel like. This tragedy ranks highest amongst events which induce the severest grief, stress or breakdown. For some people, the grief is never resolved. And no bereaved parent will forget the child. Put more graphically, it was the supreme sacrifice the Lord asked of Abraham. And when Abraham prepared to obey and laid Isaac on the altar, the angel of the Lord stayed him, 'For now I know that thou fearest God, seeing that thou has not withheld thy son, thine only *son*, from me.'

The grief syndrome here is as for any major bereavement, but it is accentuated not just by the strength of the suffering parents' love, but also by the child having been their unique creation. It is accentuated, too, by the degree of their involvement, their hope for the future and the sacrifice put into the child's upbringing.

It is often assumed that the shared grief of the parents is more tolerable than when there is only a single mourner. In their deep sorrow they can comfort each other in a way that other people cannot do. This can be true, but shared fate and shared grief are not always easy to handle. The two opposing feelings of sadness and anger can be split between the partners. One partner may be left carrying all the sadness, the other all the anger. The behaviour of one can feel intolerable to the other just because the feeling which engenders it is repudiated: 'Why is she so angry? Anger doesn't help.' 'Why does he just mope? I cannot bear his tears.' Similarly, a rift can occur between couples when one partner experiences all the grief and the other, trying not to sink into despair, tries to keep cheerful and buoyant.

Grief is particularly acute when the child has carried too many of the parents' projections, expressing what neither of them could express for themselves. (First and second children in families are those most often required to do this. Later children usually escape more lightly.) Again, grief may be exceptionally intense when feelings about the child have been ambivalent, resentment at having to meet needs having outweighed the joy.

One of the dangers in grieving for a lost child is the tendency to enshrine the memory and possessions (often in the room that was the child's bedroom) to the exclusion of continuing joy and investment in the remaining children who are *alive*. Probably the younger and more innocent the lost child, the easier it is to do this, if not in the bedroom at least in the mind. Even without the shrine, many siblings of deceased children grow up to be subdued people, ashamed of owning their own life and liveliness after their brother or sister has lost theirs. It can affect their whole outlook and, therefore, their whole life.

CHILDLESSNESS

Because the fundamental purpose of parenthood is the promotion of life and continuance of the species, procreation has archetypal significance for the individual and society. The motif of the 'divine child' abounds in myth and fairy-tale and in the dreams of many people in 1988. And, no doubt, it is likely to be present in the dreams of many of those alive in 2050.

It is, perhaps, because of this archetypal significance that so many people demonstrate such an insistent need to create a child in their own image – a child that could not be produced by anyone else. In this sense, every parent, however modestly endowed, can be said to be a creative artist.

Marriage and child-bearing remain linked in most people's minds. There is a general expectation that those who marry will have children and that those who want children will marry. Folk wisdom holds that children create a family and in such statements as 'They have got a family', or 'Their family has left home', the word 'family' means children. There is also the view, not necessarily supported by fact, that children help to maintain a marriage and ensure stability. Children are thought to be a potential source of emotional satisfaction. They make effort and sacrifice worth while; and they give a sense of immortality: 'Die single and thy image dies with thee.'

The demographic figures support the general expectation that people want to reproduce themselves.[9] At present babies are popular. Although the proportion of only children is rising, the general fertility rate in this country is higher than in any of our European counterparts except Ireland. Yet family size is falling here too, 1.8 children being the average number that women choose to have. Predictions made confidently in the 1980s of a rise in the general fertility rate are now more questionable, but do not detract from the assertion that children continue to be a fundamental aspect of the expected futures of most couples. Despite the changing role of married women and the number of them in paid employment, there is only a very small percentage of women who expect to remain childless; fewer women live through their childbearing years without giving birth than was the case sixty years ago, and nine out or ten couples will have children. While the birth-rate for the under-twenties is projected to decrease slightly, and for those between twenty and twenty-four to remain stable, that for women over twenty-five is expected to rise until at least the end of the century.

Against this background of expectation the infertile first have to encompass the shock of finding themselves potentially childless. Very few of the sterile have knowledge of their condition before their first attempt to conceive. When they learn of their infertility, they not only become part of a minority group, but in our pro-natalist society, with the folklore and ideology we have described, they have to face the spoken and unspoken question, 'When are you going to have children?', not 'Are you going to have children?' It is still difficult for the voluntary and involuntary childless to say 'Never'. The grief is not made easier by their being a source of envy to the child-encumbered who are not enjoying parenthood. The childless remain a reminder of lost opportunities (real or imagined) and a challenge to prevailing values.

While fertility investigations are going on, a couple can still have hope. Women seem to be at their lowest ebb before they dare to consult their GP, men while awaiting a diagnosis. The stress of the mixture of hope and hopelessness is accentuated by the evaluation and treatment, which are often time-consuming, painful, threatening, repetitive, tedious, sometimes insensitive and often inconclusive. The question of whose bodily fault – his or mine, hers or mine – looms large. Feelings of frustration, inadequacy, fright, isolation, anger and guilt are common. The wives normally show more overt emotion than their husbands, although it is the husbands who are sometimes more seriously threatened, perceiving the doctor, when male, as a potent competitor who may do what they have failed to do – impregnate their wives.

Once a verdict of irreversible infertility is given, the grief needs to be lived through. Counsellors who work in fertility clinics have found the sequence of grief to be similar to that following bereavement by death. But how difficult to grieve for the loss of a 'never-to-be-born' infant. How do you grieve for someone who has never been? As in all loss, part of the grief is for the lost image of the self – in this case, the image of potential parent.

The intensity of the grief will vary according to the personal meaning invested in creating and parenting. For Amelia and Paul Blackburn, the unfulfilled expectation was a severe disappointment. They were saddened and, for some months, lethargic before recovering their normal energy and zest for life. For Christopher and Muriel Chester, the loss was way beyond disappointment, and their grief radically coloured their lives for several years. Even when they came through it and found compensations, they remained deeply saddened. For Ann Hurst, the loss felt like total defeat in her long-standing rivalry with her by now prolific sister. Her husband, James, was left with a sense of acute discomfort, of being different, even to the extent of feeling an outcast from society.

The couples who are most likely to come through their grief and find compensation are those who together actively wanted a child and who *together* recognize their *shared* fate. Yet as we have mentioned before in this chapter, when there are two chief mourners, shared fate and shared grief are not easy to handle. There is a tendency for opposing feelings of sadness and anger to become split between the partners.

People who are afraid to grieve may deny the fact of their infertility and troop from one clinic to another, putting increasing pressure on the next *expert* to do what all others have failed to do. Amongst these may be some couples who too quickly resort to artificial insemination by donor, IVF or embryo transfer without first considering the full implications for themselves and the child so conceived.

Other couples may displace the normal anger of grief on to the medical profession whose expertise failed to help them. Others may use their anger more productively in the service of some cause, directing the anger on to objects, policies or institutions. Some may, sadly, make their partner the butt. They may eventually divorce or, if unable to part, may remain in the violent conflict so vividly portrayed in Albee's play *Who's Afraid of Virginia Woolf?* Yet others may take the anger into themselves, later becoming depressed, having their condition described as 'delayed grief reaction'.

And then there are those couples who are not given a clear diagnosis – the 10 per cent of those who attend a clinic for whom the aetiology of the infertility cannot be identified. It is now widely accepted that emotional factors can be a contributory cause of involuntary childlessness and that tension can reduce fertility through endocrine and other metabolic pathways.

Ambivalence about pregnancy and parenthood can be expressed through infertility, the conscious wish to parent counteracted by an unconscious fear. The problem may be about commitment to a child or part of a wider fear of commitment in any relationship. But children cannot be disposed of as readily as marriage partners. People who are highly ambivalent often attend fertility clinics, sometimes one after the other, but tend to reject the treatment or advice which is offered, finding a variety of excuses to explain why they could not follow the prescribed routine.

Women, more than men, tend to use therapy to get in touch with their underlying conflicts. They may well have had a stormy relationship with their own mother, need to be different from her and fear that they might harm a child of their own. In these instances, therapy normally needs to be long term and is rarely available within the National Health Service in Britain.

Some couples create and use conflict in their marriage as a defence against an underlying fear of pregnancy or parenthood. They clearly state that they cannot start a pregnancy while their marriage is so turbulent – so turbulent that onlookers wonder why they have not separated years ago. They may ask for help to get their marriage on to a more even keel, but every time things seem to be getting a little better and the issue of children can again come to the fore, the turbulence is re-created so that, once more, the question of parenting can be put into abeyance.

Some couples conceive surprisingly quickly once they start attending a fertility clinic and even before a diagnosis is made. This may be related to their having taken the initiative in finding out about their condition and taking the problem seriously, rather than just leaving the matter 'in the hands of the gods'. They may, as it were, have dealt with their own ambivalence. Or it may be that what is important is the time, attention and willingness of someone who helps distil the personal meaning for them, as individuals, of bearing and rearing children, or of failing so to do.

HANDICAP AND ILLNESS

There is much grief for people who bear a handicapped child, the handicap apparent at birth or soon after. Such is the normal wish for a 'perfect' healthy baby, it can, if the handicap is not too grossly obvious, be tempting to deny that something is wrong. One study on this subject found a distinct difference between the behaviour of the families who made the necessary adjustment in their lives and that of those who failed to do so.[10] In the former group, the family allowed the mother, as the chief mourner, to retreat, at times to cry, perhaps to rage, and to have extra sleep. Fathers took on additional chores and care of other children, but every so often they hauled the mothers back into the fold with the implicit message that life had to go on. These families were very busy. They insisted on a second medical opinion and sought out other families in a similar situation, gaining both knowledge and support. They used any services which were available. In contrast, the second group failed to acknowledge the crisis and grief, but remained apathetic. It did not help when the fathers tried to share the chores. Often an insecure wife and mother found this too threatening and derided the efforts.

Beyond the shock and initial grief, there may be years and years of care required for a child who cannot walk or move, hear or talk, or reach the normal milestones until many years later than normal children if at all. There may be the most difficult choice to make between using all the family resources to continue care with the help of what are often totally inadequate community services, and parting with the child to be looked after in a special school or institution. In our present medical and social climate the latter course may not be so easy, as the current emphasis is on the rights of the handicapped to lead as normal a life as possible in the community and be integrated with the able.

Not only may parents find little time and attention for each other, but able children, like siblings of deceased children, may suffer from lack of attention and assume a premature maturity in helping their parents with the burden of care.

In Chapter 5 we mentioned the sexual problems that can arise after the birth of a disabled child. Tragic consequences of heterosexuality can lessen desire. This is most likely to happen when the tragedy is an external confirmation of some old, sometimes unconscious, fear; 'beset by the sins of the fathers', a couple feel guilt and a conviction that past deeds have had to be punished. Or a deep-seated feeling of lack of worth may be confirmed by the manifestation of handicap.

Severe long-term illness in one partner obviously puts an immense strain on a marriage. When the body slowly degenerates, and the victim becomes more and more helpless, the partner and the whole family need to find additional practical and emotional resources. Many, perhaps most, families manage this in a way they could not have envisaged at the start of the illness. But divorce is not unheard of in these circumstances. To the outsider it seems so cruel for a seriously ill person to be deserted. But some people are particularly frightened of illnesses, doctors and hospitals. A variety of experiences or early fantasies may play into this. These people may have severe separation anxieties, and, if the illness is life-threatening, heralding the final separation of death, they may desert before they are deserted.

Roy Benson married Maureen, who was severely handicapped, when they were both in their twenties. He wanted to look after her and had no confidence in his ability to woo and win an able-bodied person. He was deprived, insecure and previously had led an isolated life. Their marriage worked well for fifteen years, both of them much satisfied with each other. Then Roy needed to go into hospital for a major, but not normally life-threatening, operation. Duly recovered and able to resume his care of Maureen he found that nothing he could do for her was right. She could not bear that he was the one who had been ill. Her fear that he might die and desert her was quite unconscious and expressed itself only through her bitter attacks on him. She could not forgive him for the betrayal of his six weeks' absence. The basis on which their marriage had worked so well – he the carer, she the cared-for – was shaken to its foundations. He seriously thought about leaving her, although he was frightened of being on his own without anyone to care for.

Severe illness inevitably controls the movements and actions of family members. People whose childhood has been seriously affected by an ill or disabled parent over many years usually acquire a precocious maturity. Because the foundations of this apparent maturity are not strong enough to carry the weight of responsibility required, and deep dependency needs have not been met as much as they would normally have been, this veneer may break down in adulthood. These people may remain very frightened of expressing their dependency needs and have little faith that they can be the one who can be looked after without themselves becoming totally disabled.

Some insecure invalids can unconsciously use an illness to control their partner and their children beyond the actuality of their needs, as did Bertrand Browning, described earlier in this chapter. And this drive to control does not always arise from the fear of being left in their invalid state. It can be based on a much deeper insecurity and need to have people predictably on call where they are wanted, and close by. Some or all of these factors are likely to have been part of the original unconscious covenant between the partners. Their accentuation in illness is then felt less as a betrayal than it would be by people whose original covenant did not demand control or continuous physical proximity.

REDUNDANCY AT WORK

People who have grown up or worked for much of their adult life in the historically unique period of high employment between the end of the last war and the mid 1970s will, in the main, have taken work and employment for granted. With this expectation, redundancy, or the threat of it, can be deeply disturbing.

Loss of job incorporates multiple losses beyond the obvious ones of loss of pay packet, adequate income and consumer power. Work is a means of exercising skill, organizing time, structuring the day, obtaining distance from marriage partner and children and finding companionship. In our work-orientated society, it is also a way of defining the self, acquiring status and experiencing a sense of achievement.

In addition, loss or threatened loss of job rouses a very primitive anxiety in most people, presumably because, since the beginning of time, work has been connected in the mind with physical survival and, therefore, with psychological stability.

This primitive anxiety can also be experienced as a threat of the loss of love. As Melanie Klein has explained in relation to the first few months of life, food and love are experienced as coming from the same source:

> Security was first afforded to us by our mother, who not only stilled the pangs of hunger, but also satisfied our emotional needs and relieved anxiety. Security attained by satisfaction of our essential requirements is, therefore, linked with emotional security.[11]

The definition of redundant in the *Oxford Dictionary* is 'superfluous'. This word will have greater effect on the inner world of a person who lacks confidence in his innate loveableness than on that of a person sure of his own worth. The former will find confirmation of his image of his own worth-lessness. The latter may be severely shaken in his belief that he as an individual is not superfluous, but will have the basic resource with which to recover from the shock.

Some people can use their redundancy to good effect and some years later look back and say it 'made' them, forcing them to enter another type of job which suited them better, to go it alone as self-employed, to adjust to alternative ways of using their still abundant energy or to adapt to a more leisured life as many people do on normal retirement.

Many people, however, fail to use this crisis to their own advantage and become stuck, as it were, in a chronic state of grief, unable to move through it to invest themselves in alternative pursuits. Grief, as well as poverty, prevents them from finding alternative satisfactions. They develop a debilitating inertia and speak of their depression, boredom, laziness and utter despair. Physical and mental symptoms often increase. In Britain one study showed a 20 per cent increase in consultations with the GP and 60 per cent in hospital outpatient attendance.[12] Recent studies of suicide and deliberate self-harm show an over-representation of unemployed people compared with the general population.[13] One report plotted the link between poverty, unemployment and death-rates.[14] Divorce statistics show that overall the rate is highest for unemployed people – double the national average in each age group.[15]

Strange as it may seem, for some people unemployment may be a more devastating experience than bereavement. In our recent study of the impact of unemployment on marriages,[16] we found that for many people work was a more important means of maintaining their sense of identity than were their love relationships. In addition, there was the ambivalence (always a factor in intensifying grief) with which many had regarded their jobs, both hating them and yet unable to do without them. Finally there was the factor of shame which intensified the grief, a shame presumably deepened by the general work ethic, and the attitude of some politicians and some of the employed that the unemployed are natural scroungers, idlers and layabouts. The unemployed are unlikely to admit their predicament to the doctor or the few people they meet socially. Curtains are often kept drawn and doorbells left unanswered.

The mourning process after loss of job is a complex one. The unclosed system makes it difficult for people to get on with and through the business of grief. Death is final. Unemployment may or may not be. The unemployed receive contrary economic and political messages: industry is recovering, get on your bike and search; society is moving into a post-industrial phase and technological change means that there will never be enough jobs to go round. Many unemployed remain in a state of temporary or permanent suspension.

After loss of a loved one, many people say that it was their job that kept them sane. The structure of work serves as a prop, a means of getting through the day. It provides some containment for the distress or some temporary relief from it. When it is the job that is lost, the domestic sphere may not be as capable of providing an ordered structure, a purpose beyond the self or relief from a mixture of feelings. Without work and going out to work, people are thrown back on their own resources and those of their immediate family, but with reduced finances and, therefore, less means to distance themselves when a breathing space is needed.

To use Eliot's words, 'The morning that separates' is important in most marriages. Either both partners leave to go their separate ways for eight hours or so, or one leaves and the other stays at home looking after children and house. In circumstances of enforced premature retirement from work in youth or middle age, the problem of increased or constant togetherness can be immense. 'Oh, I would love him to go off and get out from under my feet,' is a common *cri de coeur*. The problem of too much togetherness is obviously increased in small, inadequate or impoverished housing. It is particularly difficult for those who are having difficulty in handling their joint grief for all the incurred losses.

Wives are also affected by loss of income, a changed standard of living and loss of the status which their husband's job provided for them. They have often lost the image of the man they originally chose to marry – a steady worker and a good provider. This can be felt as betrayal. There are two grievers, and as we have stated before, married grief is difficult to handle.

Unemployment necessitates a reassignment of roles in the domestic sphere. Although most partners expect this to be so, each may have different ideas as to what the reassignment should be. And if the couple have led mainly segregated lives with a very clear division of role and task, it can often be difficult for them to start sharing.

Excessive house renovation by the redundant employee is a common phenomenon – job creation. But what does he do when there is little left to renovate or no cash with which to do it? Babies may be created, despite the extra financial drain when resources are short. Without the boost to potency provided by employment, sexuality in bed can become imperative and leave wives feeling used and exhausted. Arthur Ryan and his wife, Jane, kept busy in bed until she conceived, but he blew his top one morning when he found Jane had laid the fire. This activity, normally his job, had been in his eyes the only other remaining vestige of his masculinity.

Other men find they lose their potency. This can happen even when redundancy and a golden handshake have been taken voluntarily. We have mentioned several latent functions of work. But we can add another to the list which is of a different order. Many jobs allow for the sublimation (diversion) of primitive impulses into a socially acceptable form. As Freud said, 'Work is the most practical and obvious of all sublimations.' But he was not the first person to write about this. Ovid advised, 'You who seek a termination of your passion, attend to your business; . . . soon will voluptuousness turn its back on you.'

When any strong impulse is contained or given a useful channel or expression through a job, it is less likely to prove destructive within the intimacy of marriage. With no channel of expression outside the marriage, it can often be properly feared as too overwhelming or destructive within it. This type of unconscious fear can result in sexual impotence.

When made redundant, many men feel robbed – robbed of one of the main threads of their life and therefore of their masculinity. 'Robbery' is one of the most vivid images presented by the unemployed. The British miners in the long strike of 1984–5 often used the word 'stolen'. But it is not just the husbands who feel robbed. Sometimes, in an attempt to deal with this feeling, a husband steals his wife's job.

Edna Murray was a friendly, placid woman when her husband, Gordon, was working. Two years after his redundancy, she was a wreck of her former self, edgy and fidgety, with deep rings under her eyes. 'I have no life of my own,' she said. Gordon now organized everything in the house. He insisted on 'helping', as he called it, but actually supervised as he had done in his job. He often changed her milk order, or in the supermarket put products she had chosen back on the shelf and substituted others for them. Sadly, she said she wished she were young enough to have another baby. At least he could not steal that job from her.

How can this sort of behaviour be explained? We believe that 'robbery' is an expression of unconscious envy. As we mentioned earlier, envy is a very primitive emotion and is never entirely mitigated even in the best of upbringings. In a child it is often expressed symbolically by theft, usually in the home and from the mother, not with delinquent intent, but as if it were a taking by right.

If jobs are felt to be a 'right', in terms of a basic need for physical and emotional nourishment, it is not surprising that when jobs are suddenly taken from people the word 'stolen' is used so often, and so much unconscious robbery then takes place. When Gordon Murray was made redundant, he was unaware of his envy of his wife whose job had not been stolen. Apparently envy was not a major factor in this marriage while Gordon was working. But just as blaming or violence can sometimes be an attempt at communication, so too can envy be enacted when words fail to describe an uncomfortable feeling, often that of despair. If the impulse cannot be described, it is expressed in action. Gordon Murray, in his attempt to get closer to Edna in his distress, took over her work as he felt others had taken over his. He tried to make her experience what it felt like to be him.

Envy is often a component of violent behaviour. The high divorce rate of the unemployed which we mentioned earlier is characterized by the fact that unemployed husbands are more likely to be divorced for 'intolerable behaviour' than the average husband divorced by his wife, but only half as likely to have committed adultery.[17] Yet the sense of betrayal in such marriages can be just as keen. Unemployed husbands often feel betrayed by their previous employer and the economic and political systems. Financially less secure, they are unconsciously threatened with lack of love. In their turn, they betray their wives through their envy, frustrated behaviour and inability to move through their grief.

INFIDELITY

The degree to which people can feel betrayed by their marriage partner depends on the covenant and troth, spoken and unspoken, that the couple made with each other in the first place. It depends, too, on their continuing degree of involvement with each other. Commitment in marriage implies some trust and dependence on another at many levels. But in attempting to understand people's behaviour when they feel betrayed – wounded is the word so often used – we need to take account of the idealization of the in-love state and the weight of expectation in the conscious and unconscious hopes vested in the chosen partner to make better what was felt to be wrong in the past, including earlier betrayals.

Chapters 2 and 3 suggested that we have all experienced a series of betrayals as we have been expected to relinquish our infantile omnipotence and grow up beyond the harmonious whole that can for a time be enjoyed by a baby with his main caring figure. We all have to learn that there is no Garden of Eden, that life is unfair, promises are fallible and external forces can prevail against the best of intentions. One of the many betrayals we, as marital therapists, hear about is that experienced by very deprived people in their loss of innocence in marriage. The more deprived a person is, the more he tends to idealize the loving state, and the more difficult it is for him to accept that the partner is a separate and different person who does what the other wants not necessarily because of a perfect mutuality, but because of an adult ability to make a sacrifice.

The fact that betrayal is something that concerns us all is borne out by the number of modern as well as classical novels that use betrayal as a major theme. It is the *leitmotiv* of E. M. Forster's novels, all of them imbued with a deep pessimism, incidents of rejection, abandonment and direct betrayal. Even the too-good-to-be-true Mrs Moore in *Passage to India* finally turns traitor when she refuses to help Aziz and Miss Quested after the incident in the Marabar Cave. James Stanaway, in Penelope Lively's *Road to Lichfield*, 'turned and looked at his wife. "I am sorry," he said, "that I seem to have kept something of myself back from you. That is, perhaps, the shabbiest betrayal of all." '

The word betrayal, as we mentioned previously, is meaningless if there is no element of trust, just as trust has no meaning in a situation of certainty. In Jung's terms, we are speaking of the 'principle of opposition'. It was only when Samson told Delilah 'all his heart' that he finally put himself in a vulnerable position and she was able to fulfil her intention of betraying him to the Philistines.

Philip and Irma Prentice had both been promiscuous before they met. They were amazed that, in contrast to previous sexual relationships in which a grand passion had always dwindled from its early height, their love had grown slowly and had been a different experience. This new loving had grown from an early liking. Irma was thrilled when one of her dreams, very different from earlier ones she had recounted to her therapist, confirmed her newly emerging conscious ability to depend on and trust Philip. A few days later she was very upset after what she called a 'few bad days' for them. 'After that dream,' she said, 'I felt quite betrayed. I do not think it is too strong a word.' The 'few bad days' occurred just before they were having to separate for some weeks, the first separation they had had to handle since they started living together. Trust had come into their lives, but also the possibility of betrayal, sexual infidelity, even total abandonment. Could they sustain their new love through the enforced separation? Clearly, both of them had become quite anxious about this.

Despite the fact that sexual 'freedom' is maintained by some couples, sexual fidelity not being part of the original covenant for them, the majority of people, it seems, do ask for and expect fidelity. Attitude surveys in this country and overseas continue to rate faithfulness and monogamy among the highest values couples hold in relation to marriage, despite their widespread pre-marital sexual experience and the unprecedented opportunities for extra-marital sexual liaisons.

When trust has been betrayed, people feel forsaken, abandoned, wounded – stabbed in the back – and in the anguish the talion law can quickly come into operation. The temptation is to fight back, to wound as one has been wounded. *Revenge* with a capital R can rule the day in an attempt to settle old scores, as anyone who has witnessed an acrimonious divorce can testify.

When people cannot bear to let themselves know about their anguish – and the strength of the anguish will depend on the strength of their involvement – they may use the defence of denial and insist that there never was any trust in the first place. Like the fox in Aesop's fable who walked away from the grapes he could not reach 'with an air of dignity and unconcern, remarking, "I thought those grapes were ripe, and now I see they are quite sour"', they deny what has gone before. Sometimes cynicism takes over, cheapening as well as denying the value of previous love. All love becomes a cheat, a fraud or a trap. But in the refusal to live their own suffering, they alienate themselves from their past and all that has been of value in it. In doing this they end up betraying themselves.

These are all negative outcomes. There are positive ones too. Just as trust is the forerunner of betrayal, forgiveness can be its sequel. But how hard this is. The problem of forgiveness, or the paradox of it, is that one is not really forgiving if one can easily forgive. When deeply hurt, one cannot forgive to order.

The word only becomes meaningful when it involves daring to trust again. There can be no forgiveness on the part of one partner, if there is no atonement by the other. As Hillman has said, one of the paradoxes of betrayal 'is the fidelity which both betrayed and betrayer keep, after the event, to its bitterness'.[18] Only within the environment of the bitterness which was created can atonement and forgiveness have any reality.

The betrayal of sexual fidelity has many causes. As we mentioned in Chapter 4, some people are not able to create excitement in their marriage and can only enjoy passionate sex outside it. Others may have to remain perpetual Don Juans to reassure themselves of their sexual potency. Yet others, unsure of their own loveability, may use an affair to get themselves forgiven and reclaimed.

Some people stay in an unsatisfactory marriage, putting up with their dissatisfaction until they have the additional motive of an attraction to another who, they feel, provides them with what they are missing in their marriage. Without this spur they may be afraid of being on their own; or they may decide that the disruption caused to the children will be too great. With it (although they may often be torn between their lover and the needs of the children, or sometimes between the lover and their original partner) they may finally use the affair to start a new partnership. Others may use an affair to leave a marriage, but with no lasting intention of settling down with the lover (a 'transitional person' as such lovers have been called).[19] In these instances the third parties, used as transitional lovers, are often amazed by what has 'hit' them as they are swept off their feet. The leaving partner takes all the initiatives, makes them feel so wanted, but leaves them so out of control before deserting them as they have their spouse.

This type of transitional affair may also be used to 'rock the boat' of a marriage rather than to end it. One dissatisfied partner, wanting to change the original covenant but unable to get the other to hear his dissatisfaction, may act in response to the frustration. In these instances people are often surprised by their own uncharacteristic behaviour when they sweep into an affair. Only later do they realize they needed to shock their spouse into facing up to the underlying difficulties in the relationship. Other people are more aware of the purpose behind their actions and are quite explicit that an affair is just a symptom of other difficulties which should have received attention before.

There are many conscious and unconscious meanings and motives behind infidelity. It can often be difficult to understand what lies behind a series of compulsive but unsatisfactory affairs. The explanation may be linked with significant anniversaries. Sad events which were not properly mourned in the past can leave people inexplicably depressed on their anniversary. The sadness may be unbearable. In attempting to ward off depression they may seek excitement or release of tension through an affair.

The marriage of Liam and Edna Martin had had its ups and downs over the years, but overall they had remained pleased with each other. They did not have the difficulties that some people experience when their youngest child left home. Laughing at themselves and their rejuvenation, they delighted in having more time for themselves and each other. Two years later, however, in their words, 'all went flat' for them, despite having much to look forward to, including a first grandchild. Liam embarked on a series of 'meaningless' affairs, as he described them, which shook them both. Why did this happen now when fidelity had not been a problem in the past? The compulsion behind the meaningless affairs was a defence against the flatness. The underlying depression related to a stillborn child which, if born, would have been twenty-one years old. As the therapist commented, 'A ghost, or the felt last child was due to leave home.' 'Nonsense,' they said in disbelief. 'We haven't thought of that for years.' Yet it was Liam Martin who brought up the subject in the consulting room twenty-two years after the stillbirth;

speaking of his compulsive affairs, he was the one who made this strange juxtaposition of subject. It seemed his unconscious served him well that afternoon. Focusing the discussion on that earlier loss eradicated the compulsion behind the affairs. Trust took longer to resume.

An unconscious fear of incest or incestuous feelings can drive some men into affairs when a lovely teenage daughter, so like the wife when first courted and married, is becoming a sexual paragon. In these instances, the distressed wife is left baffled why, when the sexual relationship and marriage generally felt good, her husband needed to find another woman. The affair may well break up the marriage, but in these instances it is the daughter more than the wife who is 'divorced'.

When one partner has a prolonged affair and the other partner objects but continues to suffer it, even – wittingly or not – aiding and abetting what is happening, both partners may have a problem about triangles. The betrayed spouse may have as much investment in the affair as the partner who finds the lover. Ada Tompkins was vociferous about her husband's lover, but remained fascinated by her, wanted to know every detail of the association and on some occasions even drove him to the lover's flat. The lover, fed up and disillusioned in her earlier hope that she would finally win Jim Tompkins and lure him out of his marriage, eventually ended the affair. Jim suffered some feelings of loss, but soon felt the whole thing could be put behind them if only Ada would do the same. But Ada could not let go of her sense of outrage and betrayal, nor her curiosity. It was she who kept the ex-lover alive in the marriage. This was not just an inability to forgive, hard as that often is. It had more to do with her own latent homosexuality. Unable to recognize this, the nearest she could get to the bed of another woman was through her husband's action. Anxiety about latent homosexuality can underlie a lot of affairs which then become the product of a constant need to prove heterosexuality.

The threat of AIDS, with its high fatality rate, has added a literal threat to life to the emotional wound of the partner's unfaithfulness. The officially recorded figure of the number infected with the virus, of whom a large proportion can be expected to develop the disease in four or five years' time, was in September 1987, 8,016. However the real number was thought at that time to be as high as 30,000, even 40,000[20] owing to people now avoiding a test because of the implications. As yet there is no major epidemic, but without a vaccine, treatment or a change in sexual behaviour, there well could be.

To date, only seventeen women have contracted the disease although over three hundred men and women have been infected with the virus through heterosexual contact. But, if one partner of a couple carries the virus, the medical, practical and social implications are enormous, and range from the problem of obtaining medical and life insurance to social ostracism.

When infection is confirmed, whom do you dare tell? From whom can you seek support? Although the public are repeatedly informed that infection is only through anal or vaginal intercourse, or through intravenous injection, fear of contagion is strong enough for many people to keep their distance. AIDS is the new leprosy. The national campaign to encourage people to use condoms for sexual intercourse with any partner whose 'state of health is uncertain' seems to have had little effect. It is difficult to understand the irrational fear of contagion on one hand and, on the other, blithe disregard of the real dangers among some heterosexuals. That many people are still taking an immense risk in the face of this threat raises the question of whether AIDS is a less frightening prospect for some than the fear of committed intimacy with one partner. Reason counts for little when the unconscious motivations we have described in this chapter come into play.

'And what about our marriage?' asked the young wife in a television play, when she, having learnt of her husband's affair and infection, attended for a test. 'That depends on what your marriage meant in the first place,' the doctor replied.

And what the marriage meant in the first place will determine the reaction of one partner when the other's affair is disclosed. When people find their faith has been betrayed by the sexual infidelity of their partner, they may be beset by a welter of primitive emotions: severe separation anxiety, paralysing feelings of helplessness and insecurity caused by the threat of abandonment or the exposed emotional distances; a sense of isolation and loss of identity now that the previous view of the self as a partner in a happy marriage no longer holds true; jealousy and fury with the third party. With this degree of upset, it can be difficult to behave rationally, and particularly to decide whether to fight for a marriage by fair means or foul, or to relinquish it with good or bad grace. Strength of feeling may overcome any rational consideration or attempt to understand why the affair has happened and one's own part in it. Initially it may feel that repair is impossible. However, many marriages do survive the shaking of their foundations, but this may mean hard work on the part of both partners and much forgiveness and atonement before trust can be restored. In the next chapter we describe the problems inherent in ending a marriage when this seems the most likely outcome of a broken troth.

8. Parting Company

The departure of love is seldom an abrupt event in marriage. It is, rather, a gradual erosion which occurs over years as a result of neglect. Parting company is a process which may be triggered by a traumatic event, a breach of trust or a disappointment. It may be the consequence of one partner outgrowing the other, or of each immersing themselves in different and disconnected lives. It is a bleak time. 'Alas my love is gone, I am alone; it is winter,' wrote Walter de la Mare of the experience. There need be no actual separation for couples to part company, only a growing indifference towards each other; the winter of marriage does not necessarily end in divorce.

Occasionally the loss of a partner will come unexpectedly. Sudden desertion will rupture the bond of physical presence which is taken so much for granted and which holds couples together in a web of secure familiarity. In the face of an inescapable absence, it is no longer possible to rub along in the usual way. Some of the routines and rituals of everyday life become irrelevant – even crazy – when continued in the face of radically altered circumstances. But even when marriage is terminated abruptly, the process of parting company takes time, and sometimes a very long time. As after death, there are many Queen Victorias erecting mausoleums to their Prince Alberts to cushion themselves from the painful realization of being alone. Unlike bereavement, however, the memories preserved and engaged with can be bitter when one partner has *chosen* to leave the other.

This chapter is not about the loss of a partner through death, although we shall be drawing on our knowledge of the stages of mourning through which the bereaved pass in order to understand the reactions of couples who part company in other ways. Rather, we shall be considering the predicament of men and women who feel they are in an unsatisfactory marriage and wondering what to do about it. Frequently marriage is experienced as a prison or an empty shell. In this situation we need to ask what it is that couples wish to escape from, or why they feel drawn in a new direction.

ASSESSING THE KNOWN

THE CAGED BIRD

Jeanie White married when she was nineteen and expecting her first child. Her husband, John, was five years older, better educated, and from a higher social drawer than Jeanie. He had traditional views about the roles of men and women in marriage. His protective, and sometimes paternal, attitude towards his wife had been very attractive to her in the early stages of their relationship. Her parents had divorced when she was fourteen, and as a result she had had to take a major share of responsibility for looking after the home while her mother went out to work. John seemed to offer some relief from these burdens, despite his traditional views about home life and his part in ensuring their marriage started out with the responsibilities of parenthood. As time went by, and Jeanie became the mother of two children, she felt increasingly constrained by life at home and wanted to break out.

One event symbolized for her the source of her oppression. When the younger child had started at playgroup, Jeanie told John that she wanted to find a job. He objected to the idea, saying that it was not financially necessary and that she had enough to do at home. For several months she resentfully accepted this, until a friend brought to her attention an opportunity she felt she could not ignore. Only after she had secured the job did she tell her husband and he was then very angry. The distance between them increased. John took to sniping at her, criticizing her performance as a housewife and mother. Jeanie, tired from running the home and holding down a job, became bitter about the lack of support she received from John. Mutual feelings of resentment made it difficult to talk about their different points of view. Instead, John became the recriminating parent and Jeanie felt like a guilty but rebellious child.

However, a change was taking place in their relationship. Jeanie became stronger as a result of her contacts outside the home and this changed the way she perceived John. At times she felt his demands and claims on her were like having a third child in the family. Rather than feeling constrained by an oppressive parent, she felt burdened by another demanding child. Her sense of being trapped started her thinking about ways of leaving the marriage. Some years later she made the move. Looking back, she realized she had prepared the ground for leaving over a period of six or seven years. When the opportunity arose she took it, taking her children with her to her mother's home and leaving a note behind for John to explain what she had done and why.

Jeanie was conscious of several constraints which she saw as being imposed by John, and which she wanted to shrug off. She wanted to escape from the kind of relationship where she was fixed as a child who needed to have parental approval for all she did. She wanted to leave the atmosphere at home where she felt guilty about attending to her own needs and interests. And she wanted to reduce the claims made on her as mother and home-maker. Her attempts to negotiate a different balance in the relationship, one which would make it less necessary for her to leave, had not been successful. The only way out seemed to her to be to leave the marriage.

It would be easy to slip into the assumption that Jeanie had been unfortunate in marrying an unbending husband who felt too threatened by her moves towards independence to offer her the support she needed. This explanation was easiest of all for Jeanie who, caught up in the situation, was bound to have a partisan view. She may have been right. But other possibilities are worth looking at.

Jeanie had, after all, *chosen* a man who was predisposed to play the role of guardian and protector, and in the early days of the marriage this had met a need in her. She had also chosen that marriage should coincide with parenthood, a substantial burden of commitment to take on at one time. In other words, it could be argued that there was a time when she had wanted a defined role and place in the family – and perhaps the child's role – as much as she later craved release from these external definitions of herself. And when the time came for her to leave it was to her mother she went, not to a friend or relative of her own generation. There might, of course, have been very good practical reasons for this choice. Our intention here is to raise the psychological possibility of separation as an enactment of Jeanie's still ambivalent relationship to those who, in her view, occupied the place of parent.

In earlier chapters we have drawn attention to the permeability of the psychological skin which separates one person from another. This per-meability allows the possibility that what is complained of in another is, in greater measure, what cannot be tolerated in oneself. 'The mind is its own place,' wrote Milton, 'and in itself can make a Heaven of Hell, a Hell of

Heaven.' We all filter what happens to us through the distorted lens of our mind's eye. If we have grown up believing the world to be an oppressive place, it is sometimes easier to engineer (quite unconsciously) situations which conform to our assumptions than to change the assumptions themselves.

So for those in Jeanie's position it is important not only to assess what is intolerable, but also to explore the possibility of there being an investment in the way things are, however much of a nonsense this might at first seem. Equally, it is important to consider whether the compulsion to make a break might be overlaid with an unacknowledged investment from one's partner. John may have been struggling as much as Jeanie to free himself from parental shackles, but in getting her to articulate the conflict, unconsciously designated her to be the one to do the breaking.

Marriage and parenthood entail commitments which can enthral, with all the ambiguities contained in that word. Marrying can be a means of jumping out of the frying-pan of an unsatisfactory home life only to land in the fire of other ties. Leaving a spouse can then become equated with leaving home, the spouse having come to assume all the properties of a restrictive parent or demanding child. Sorting out what belongs to which relationship is important if unresolved personal conflicts are not to be transferred from one context into another. Becoming independent can entail parting company not just from a partner, but, by becoming reconciled with previously disowned aspects of oneself, from the process of attribution by which each one of us protects ourselves from knowing about the parts of ourselves we dislike.

For Jeanie, the prison she wished to escape was oppressive paternalism. For others it may be depression, a lack of glamour, parsimony, spendthriftiness, coolness, violence or other expressions of passion. Whatever the outcome, the process of assessing the known includes the question, 'Is it you or is it me?' Having said that, hell on earth is seldom all of one's own making. Other people do behave badly on their own account, and it does not help to perpetuate destructive ways of relating. Each of us has a duty to ourself as well as to others. Marriages do irretrievably break down, and parting company can be a constructive solution.

THE EMPTY SHELL

Stephen and Sue Black married against their parents' wishes. It was the first major decision they took independently in their lives. Both were only children. Sue was the apotheosis of her mother's frustrated aspirations, and even at the age of twenty-four she had done little without first consulting her parents. Stephen grew up in a less ambitious atmosphere; his family was closed and unadventurous.

Sue and Stephen chose to conduct their courtship privately, and the secrecy with which they cloaked their relationship afforded a spice and excitement which had been lacking in their lives. This was the first significant relationship from which their parents had been excluded. They created an island together which was inaccessible to outsiders. Their parents reacted more and more unfavourably to being shut out, which only caused the couple to cling to each other more excitedly as if to life itself. Deteriorating relations with parents precipitated the marriage earlier than might otherwise have been the case. Sue's parents stayed away.

One year later, the marriage was flat. Sue and Stephen found themselves facing each other with nothing to say. The sexual excitement which had fuelled their courtship had abated once they were married. Each found they were looking to the other to provide the missing momentum in the marriage; neither was able to supply it. Their life together carried on in a routine and lifeless way, and both of them felt they had lost their 'oomph'. Sue became involved with a man at her work. Stephen spent an increasing amount of time at his parents' home. The flat which they had bought was often empty and began to show signs of neglect.

Empty-shell marriages come about in many different ways. For Stephen and Sue, getting married had been less about making a commitment to each other than about breaking the tie to their parents. It had been a way of declaring independence. Háving achieved their common purpose, each missed the direction which had been provided by their parents. They experienced a sense of flatness and were unable to enliven themselves or each other. Marriage had been intended to confer upon them a separate identity, but in the event it had exposed them to their own feelings of emptiness and they turned to others to fill the space.

The fear of being alone can be sufficient to drive many people into ill-considered marriages. Partnerships are then formed on the basis of a common fear which needs to be defended against, and not in the spirit of making a positive choice. 'Babes-in-the-wood' marriages rely upon a potentially hostile environment for partners to be able to find solace in each other. Yet these conditions provide the very circumstances which inhibit the separateness and independence which make satisfying relationships possible. Remove the hostile environment, and what's left?

The fear of being alone can come in many guises. For example, because marriage is a public declaration of heterosexuality it can provide a refuge for those who are uncertain or anxious about their sexual orientation. Because the norm is still for people to marry at some point in their twenties, the fear of being different, or of being 'left on the shelf', can be sufficient to motivate the commitment. Although these pressures may be less significant today than in less liberal times, they continue to apply. While they provide the shell of marriage, it is what happens subsequently which determines whether or not the shell remains empty.

Most frequently marriages become empty rather than starting out that way. In what is still the ordinary course of events, the claims of employment on men and children on women result in the 'careers' of the partners following different trajectories. As we described in Chapter 6, parenthood can mark the parting of the ways. This process of differentiation in the life history of marriage can cause problems when the experience of being separate is confused with feeling rejected. Work and child-rearing, instead of being complementary activities, may then be viewed as compensation for what has gone missing from the marriage, resulting in the creation of segregated worlds for men and women. Over the years the habit of organizing married life in separate compartments can become entrenched. Only when the children leave home, or when the man loses his job, are the couple likely to become aware of the empty space that has grown up between them.

However the emptiness in a marriage comes about, an outside relationship or opportunity can offer a tempting means of filling the space or creating something new. In responding to the external pulls, there remains the task of assessing whether one is taking flight from fears which constantly lurk beneath the surface of activity, or facing those fears head on. The decision to leave an empty-shell relationship is a courageous one when it represents a decision to grab at life instead of perpetuating the twilight of a comatose marriage.

FACING THE UNKNOWN

In weighing up the decision to part company it is not only a question of assessing the known, but also of facing one's own fears and fantasies about moving into unknown territory.

By nature we are conservative beings. This is especially true when we are very young and when we are growing old. There are good reasons for this conservatism. In Chapter 2 we described the infant's need to be securely attached in order to establish a firm footing from which to step out. Children are vulnerable. They have to rely heavily upon others to meet their physical and emotional needs. Specific people assume great importance to the children who are attached to them. If these attachment figures are absent, unreliable or unpredictable they are likely to shake the confidence of those they are there to look after. This is true in childhood more than at any other time in life. Routines and rituals provide a reassuring structure within which it becomes safe to experiment. As we grow older and more self-reliant the physical presence and influence of others becomes less important to our sense of well-being, except in times of illness or crisis. But as the years pass by, and our faculties go into decline, the value of a familiar, predictable environment is again at a premium.

The unsettling effects of change are linked with age not only through our dependence upon others but also because of our confidence in ourselves. To a large extent self-reliance depends upon how serviceable the blueprints developed within ourselves are to the situations encountered later in life. Our security derives from having drawn up internal models which prove reliable over the kind of relationships which exist between ourselves and our environment. In other words, a secure identity results from a fit between what we expect and what we experience. In the early years of life our internal models are highly volatile, very susceptible to influence and constantly undergoing revision. Although we never stop modifying these models, or trying to change the environment to conform to them as time goes by, the process becomes one of fine tuning. The longer we have relied upon our personal models, the more reluctant we are to change them. Only a major event is likely to stop us in our tracks and cause us to take stock. Because we do not make fundamental reappraisals until we have to, we become less willing to place ourselves in situations – at work, at leisure, and in our intimate relationships – where the risk of major change is high.

Parting company is never an easy option because it always involves a fundamental reappraisal and revision of identity. It becomes more difficult the longer a couple have been together, and it is especially hard for the one who is left behind. And because couples carry on their lives in the context of a social network wider than themselves, the decision to separate will seldom be welcomed by others. They, too, are likely to want their social landscape to remain unchanged.

Discounting, for the moment, the practical and social consequences of separation, there may be other factors existing just outside the realms of consciousness which can influence the decision to stay in or leave an unsatisfactory marriage. These factors include the fear of being alone, the fear of being destructive and the fear of being unloveable.

THE FEAR OF BEING ALONE

Nobody likes being lonely. As social animals dependent upon each other for survival and stimulus, we tend to gravitate towards each other. But relationships work best when we can stand being on our own and do not compulsively have to latch on to others. Being alone is somewhat different from being lonely. The capacity to tolerate one's own company is an essential part of being good company with others. Perversely, the fear of being alone (a form of separation anxiety) often prevents us from being in touch with those to whom we relate. It is not only that fear can result in attention-seeking behaviour of a self-defeating kind which drives others away, but it can also lead people to create for themselves an imaginary, private world of relationships which is defended against intrusion from outside: 'I have spread my dreams under your feet,' wrote W. B. Yeats; 'Tread softly because you tread on my dreams.'

Francis Reed feared being alone because it felt to him like going mad. To outsiders he was a genial, competent and self-contained person who seemed the least likely candidate for a nervous breakdown. However, he was driven to seek professional help, against all his instincts, by the fear that his marriage was on the rocks.

His wife, Sarah, complained that she felt increasingly out of tune with her husband. At the beginning of the marriage she had conformed with the picture of an elegant, sophisticated, worldly wise woman which she believed he had of her, but at the cost of some alienation from herself. His idealized view made her more and more depressed. When she was moody and unhappy he would greet her with a cold aloofness. When she sought to remedy the situation by enrolling in a course for horticulture (a secret ambition she had long denied herself), he was unenthusiastic. She had come to the conclusion that he was not interested in her as the person she really was, and the only solution was for her to leave the marriage.

The prospect of separation made Francis panic. As he talked about his fears he disclosed an event which had occurred during his childhood which seemed to embody what he most feared about being alone. He had been the apple of his mother's eye, until, when he was seven, a baby sister was born.

He was sure he had been delighted by the baby, and he was sure his childhood had been happy and secure. Nevertheless, he recalled a recurring dream he had had as a child in which he was piloting a spaceship which had lost contact with ground control. He remembered spending hours as a child lying on his back, staring at the sky and thinking how small he was in a huge impersonal universe. Subsequently he had devoted himself to studies which resulted in a successful career and the admiration of his family and friends.

Francis had been more unsettled by the birth of his sister than he had allowed himself to know. By preserving a rosy glow around his childhood, and by working to restore his place in people's affections, he held at bay the pain and anger of being rejected.

Psychologically, he organized his life around trying to preserve and recapture a paradise lost; he attempted to find a way back into the personal Garden of Eden from which he felt he had been ejected by his sister. Unconsciously he had encouraged his wife to step into the shoes of the elegant, admirable mother of his early childhood.

Marriage provided a context in which to play out the childhood drama, but his efforts to idealize Sarah made her depressed and alienated her from him. Francis found himself on the horns of a dilemma, wanting to distance himself from his wife's depression (which was also his own) and fearing that to do so would precipitate the separation he was so anxious to avoid. Moreover, the early years of marriage had faced him with real separations: his parents had split up and his sister had been killed in a car accident. This latter event continued to trouble him because he was haunted by an irrational feeling that he, in some way, had been responsible for her death, the sister who had displaced him all those years ago.

Francis and Sarah did part for a time. Talking about the experience, Francis used language which evoked his fear of going mad (in the sense of being angry as well as going crazy): 'It's like banging my head against a wall; I just feel it's killing me. I sometimes think I need locking up, or she does.' With therapeutic help he was able to talk about his feelings and how overlaid they were with past memories. And the experience of being apart did not drive him mad.

Separation in adult life is made all the more difficult to bear if it overlays traumatic separation in childhood. If the feelings surrounding the earlier event have not found an outlet they return to attach themselves to similar events in later life and overdetermine the reactions. Past separations may have been brought about by illness, bereavement, parental divorce or, as in Francis's case, through being displaced by another family member. Without a resolution to the conflicts engendered by past traumas, the prospect of separation in adult life can hold some of the terrors of childhood.

THE FEAR OF DESTROYING

It is not uncommon for people to fear the consequence of separation for their partner. Will she commit suicide? Will he be able to manage. Sometimes a partner who is planning to leave a marriage will suggest seeking help for the relationship as a means of ensuring that there will be someone to pick up the pieces when he or she leaves. Occasionally there are good reasons for questioning a partner's ability to manage alone. Quite often, however, the instigator is looking for help with feelings of guilt about leaving or locating in their partner fears about their own viability after the break-up.

The fears of damaging or being damaged by separation are inextricably bound up with each other. While Francis Reed thought he might go mad if he were left on his own, he also feared 'getting mad' (that is, angry) and injuring his wife, or that he might drive others mad. After all, he had 'succeeded' in ridding himself of his sister.

Of the two of them it was his wife, Sarah, who more consciously feared the consequence of damaging rather than being damaged. For some years in the marriage she had made herself physically ill by worrying about what to do; rather than registering her protest she had become depressed. It was as if she preferred to damage herself rather than take the risk of destroying Francis's self-protective dreams. The consequences of leaving were, in her mind, tantamount to destroying him.

When Sarah reviewed her life experience she gave some clues to the origins of her destructive fantasies. Her father had died when she was in her early teens, a time when she was struggling for her own independence from him and from home. Her mother reacted to the loss by becoming profoundly depressed, so that Sarah felt obliged to support her. Whenever Sarah asserted herself, her mother showed signs of becoming ill. She died of a heart attack one month after Sarah married Francis. To Sarah it seemed as if she could assert herself only at someone else's expense.

At an unconscious level, history had conspired to equate the separateness necessary for self-preservation with Sarah's own aggressive impulses which, she feared, would have damaging consequences if they found expression. She believed she could not survive within the marriage; Francis believed he could not survive outside it. She believed she could have her own separateness only at his expense. He believed he could have the marriage only at her expense. Together they shared a powerful unconscious fantasy that life for self was at the expense of death for others, and that life for others was at the expense of one's own emotional death.

In magnified form the Reeds expressed a conflict which is present in all marriages: how to survive and develop as individuals and as a partnership. In order to establish sufficient distance to make the relationship work, it sometimes feels as if an actual separation is the only way forward. In order to function as an individual it may be necessary to leave the marriage behind. The Reeds separated for a year. In that period they established sufficient separateness from each other and their own illusions to enable them to live together once again.

THE FEAR OF BEING UNLOVABLE

Low self-esteem can have a crippling effect on both marriage and the options that can be seen outside marriage. Until we are able to love ourselves we are not in a strong position to love others. If we believe that no one can want us, we may mistrust or feel contemptuous of those who show interest. Or we may feel a gratitude which inhibits making any claims of our own. We may want the security of a relationship which aspires to nothing better than a lowest common denominator; in the words of the calypso, 'If you want to be happy for the rest of your life be sure and make an ugly woman your wife.' But this is no protection against feelings of inadequacy or inferiority. Nor is it proof against an inflated self-regard which we can develop to protect us from fearing we are nobody. There is nothing so undermining of oneself as a lack of confidence in one's own acceptability and lovability.

Debbie and George Flack were both brought up in large and rather neglected families. The children were frequently left to fend for themselves in their parents' absences and, in George's case, this had led to spending part of his childhood in the care of the local authority. As the oldest in her family, Debbie spent much time looking after her younger brothers and sisters. She was rewarded for her reliability by becoming her mother's confidante and right-hand woman. She developed a way of securing attention for herself by looking after others. In contrast, George had adopted a happy-go-lucky attitude to his circumstances, having learned that things had to fall to pieces before anyone would notice.

Their young marriage started out with Debbie taking all the initiatives and looking after George, whose carefree attitude she found attractive. While this arrangement worked for a short time, Debbie later became resentful about receiving so little attention from George; and George became irritated by what he saw as Debbie's persistent nagging. Their relationship became peppered with stand-up fights which usually ended with George storming out of the house. To the outsider it came to seem as if they could barely stand being together; but equally they were unable to part.

Such 'cat and dog' marriages often conceal anxiety about becoming too close or intimate in a relationship. Intimacy requires trust and a belief that it is safe to put yourself into the hands of others. Debbie could manage a certain amount of intimacy on her terms, when she was the one doing the caring. But she expected some reciprocation if she were going to be able to let go. George was content to be looked after, but had not the confidence in himself to take responsibility for others. So they fought each other over being too demanding or too withholding. This was safer than becoming depressed. And because they feared deep inside themselves that they were 'spoiled goods', that they suffered from a basic defect which made them unacceptable to others, they could not envisage life apart.

In such marriages the developmental struggle is to come to terms with what can realistically be expected of others and of oneself. This involves coming to terms with an unchangeable past, and being able to care for the deprived child in oneself rather than expecting someone else to be the emotional 'horn of plenty'. The alternative is to remain deadlocked in an unsatisfied, but at least familiar, state of feeling badly done by. Sometimes one partner will recover confidence through a rewarding relationship or activity outside the marriage and summon up the courage to leave. The burden of failure and rejection is then compounded for the one who is left behind.

*

So far, we have been looking backwards in thinking about the influences upon those who are trying to decide whether or not to stay married. We have considered some of the psychological factors which have a bearing on the process of assessing what has been and might be if the decision to part company is made. We have not looked at the likely consequences of separation for adults and children from the basis of the experience of those who have taken this step.

THE CONSEQUENCES OF BREAKING UP

In the past ten years there has been a growing volume of research addressing the subject of separation and divorce. From this work it is possible to begin to map out the likely consequences for those affected. None of these studies can, of course, predict the exact course likely to be followed by the diverse individuals who set out on the journey, but they draw attention to the nature of the terrain, and this can prove useful. It is not our intention to try and summarize all that has been written; this has been done by others. Rather, we shall touch upon some of the main points to emerge.

THE EXPERIENCE OF THE ADULTS

Different kinds of ties are broken when people decide to separate: financial, legal, social and emotional. The rupture of established financial arrangements is of immediate concern and can be a source of worry and anger for both partners. Two households are more expensive to maintain than one. Separation and divorce frequently bring about material hardship and leave even the relatively well-off facing a fall in their standard of living.

The financial impact on women is likely to be greater than that on men. This is because men are often able to command higher earnings than women in the labour market and tend to default on maintenance arrangements, while women are frequently left with the day-to-day child-rearing responsibilities which add to their financial burdens while restricting opportunities to increase their income. Sixty per cent of women with children draw state benefit at some stage following divorce. A high proportion of the one in five children who come from families with an income below the poverty line are from broken homes. Many studies of divorcing families have drawn attention to the adverse financial consequences of divorce, and have charted the rising rate of exhaustion of women who return to work through financial necessity while continuing to be full-time mothers.[1]

Although separation does not necessarily break the legal bond of marriage, many couples will take legal advice, if not action, because so much is at stake at that time. Far-reaching decisions on parenting, financial and property matters have to be taken in a relatively short period of time. All this takes place when people are feeling at their most hurt, vulnerable and mistrustful. Safeguarding one's legal, not to say moral, rights when the fear of exploitation is high and the support received is low, are powerful drives towards activating the legal system after separation. It may then be only a relatively short step to dissolving the marriage in law.[2]

The social consequences of divorce have been likened to being despatched to a foreign country where one is confronted by new customs and practices, but without a foreign language or frontier to make it clear that a journey has been made. The lack of social support and ritual for the newly separated can be so great that it drives some into remarriage in order to recover a slot in society. Divorce is a highly unstructured change for which there is little preparation, minimal support and no sense of going anywhere except into another marriage. With the collapse of social identity can come a sense of disorientation and alienation from others.[3]

The emotional consequences of divorce are connected with the impact of severing many other ties, but the extent of distress is affected by a host of different factors. There are many losses associated with the process of parting company. A woman may lose access to the world of adult employment and the status which goes with it when her estranged husband closes this avenue of vicarious living. A man may lose the physical presence of children which daily confirms him as a father. Familiar rituals and routines come to an end. Companionship and sexual intimacy, having already waned, may finally be ended with separation, although the ambivalence associated with parting company can lead couples to fight each other one day and sleep together the next.

Perhaps most significant for the process of emotional adjustment is that hopes, expectations and projections invested by each partner in the other must end or be withdrawn. The process is comparable with bereavement, which we described in Chapter 7, and it follows a discernible and similar course.[4] There is often the same shock and disbelief about what is happening, the same restlessness and yearning interspersed with outbreaks of anger which can mingle together for months and even years. One woman described waiting for the sound of her husband's key in the door nine months after he had left her, despite the fact that she had been glad to see him go. There are others who are more ambivalent about the marriage ending and make desperate bids for a last-minute reconciliation during the legal process of divorce or even after it is finished.

Anger, yearning and protest eventually give way to sadness and depression, which herald the way to a rebuilding and re-integration of the self. In the last phase of mourning there is, therefore, the need to rebuild, identify and recover a new purpose in life. This process involves withdrawing projections and having to live with a mixture of feelings. Ambivalence is a healthy part of the after-marriage state, eventually allowing the lost partner to be seen in a more balanced light than was possible in the first acute stage of grief.

Despite these similarities, there are also differences between the experience of bereavement and that of loss of partner through divorce. The mixture of anger and sorrow which constitutes grief appears in different proportions in bereavement and divorce. Ambivalent reactions are handled differently. In the sorrow of bereavement, a partner is often idealized. Self-reproach or quick-temperedness towards others may be the only channels through which anger finds an outlet. There is a finality about death which allows no reply from the person who really matters, although an image of that person may persist and be conversed with in the privacy of the mind for many years after. In divorce, the situation is reversed. Not only is there no corpse, but there remains someone with whom an actual relationship might well persist, especially when there are children. Often the partner will be regarded as an adversary who cannot only be counted on to reply but will also constitute a threat. In these circumstances, the anger following separation frequently results in the denigration or abuse of a partner. Social conventions are likely to condone these reactions, which mask the sorrow about what has occurred. Legal institutions may oblige with a forum which is essentially adversarial and, as such, can be deeply satisfying to those who wish to fight, allocate blame and obtain public absolution. While this is a normal reaction to divorce, it would be considered bizarre and improper following bereavement.

It seems that those stricken by the death of a partner often suppress their necessary anger, while those parting company in other ways often suppress their necessary sadness. When taking far-reaching decisions about marriage and divorce it may be that we need the blindness of idealization on the one hand and denigration on the other to help us over the threshold. As one man put it: 'I have to hate her to go. I can be more civilized later on.' How much later on depends on how the divorce is managed. There are indications that the process of adjustment takes longer following divorce than bereavement. One study of divorced men reported continuing hostility and bitterness about events which had occurred eight or nine years previously.[5] Perhaps only the truly indifferent will be able to part company amicably. For the long-term consequences of separation to be positive, some acknowledgement of the fact that couples have both loved and lost is essential.

The processes we have described help to explain the kinds of symptoms commonly experienced in the first year after separation. Increased susceptibility to illness, poor concentration at work, abuse of alcohol and other drugs, occasionally violent assault and suicide, all become understandable in the context of the short-term stresses of a marriage breaking up. Divorce has been described as a major health hazard, but the degree of disturbance is hard to predict accurately for different individuals. The impact is often greatest upon the one left behind, and there is some evidence which suggests divorce hits men harder than women. Perhaps this is unsurprising in a culture where women service family relationships and express feelings on behalf of men. Disconnected from this anchorage, some men feel cast adrift in unfamiliar and unfriendly waters. The first year is likely to be the worst. The evidence indicates that for couples with children it takes between two and four years to pick up the threads of life once more.

It may seem as if the consequences of separation, as we have represented them, are one long catalogue of woes. We suspect that the majority of couples who separate will look back on their experience with confidence and conviction that they did the right thing. But we also think they would acknowledge that the process had not been easy, especially in the short term. Certainly, the weight of research suggests that parting company is a painful business and challenges the view sometimes put forward that people divorce lightly. The notion of easy divorce is even less credible when there are children involved.

THE EXPERIENCE OF THE CHILDREN

However unsettling the effects of an unhappy marriage upon children, most parents worry and feel guilty about the possible consequences for them of separation and divorce. This area has been the subject of much study in the past ten years and a general picture has begun to emerge. While it may not fit the circumstances of every individual, it can help parents to create the circumstances after marriage most likely to be helpful to their children.

It seems clear from research which has taken the children's views into account that the interests of children and parents diverge over divorce. Most children say they would have preferred their parents to stay together in an unhappy marriage rather than part, and most find it more difficult to manage the loss of a parent through divorce than death. But given that there is no alternative, the factors which most militate against a satisfactory adjustment are diminished and disrupted parenting.[6]

It is to be expected that children will make additional demands when a marriage breaks. One study estimated that between 20 per cent and 50 per cent of children show degrees of upset which require outside help at some time following the separation of their parents. Poor performance at school, aggressive or attention-seeking behaviour at home, even delinquent episodes in the community can be understood as a normal protest about being caught up in a situation not of their making. A study carried out in the United States highlighted the age differential in the behaviour of children during the acute period of response in the first year after separation;[7] the fear, regression, macabre fantasies and bewilderment of pre-school age children compared with the sadness and yearning of the six- to eight-year-olds; the anger, intense loyalty and heightened sense of right and wrong of the nine to twelves; and the anguish and withdrawal of the adolescents, who surprised the researchers by making frantic appeals to them to restore their parents' marriages. In the long run neither age nor sex were the crucial factors determining outcome, although there were indications that children who were youngest at the time of marriage break-up fared better than those who were older and had to live with troubling memories of family strife.

We have described how divorce places economic, social and psychological burdens on parents, especially in the short term when they are coming to terms with their own feelings about loss and having to make new arrangements to support their lives. The self-preoccupation which is inevitable in these circumstances is likely to leave the adults with few resources to respond to the agitation and confusion which also affect their children at this time. A mother who fluctuates between anger, tearfulness and depression is not going to be available to her children. The necessities of going out to work and maintaining social contact outside the home will mean that children spend more time in the care of temporary minders than they did before. Although divorce can bring out the best in some children, who will show remarkable maturity in dealing with the adults and taking over some of the household responsibilities, it can also mean that childhood is forfeit to a precocious move into the adult world. With luck, the period of diminished parenting will be short, allowing the children's childhood to be resumed without undue delay. But some children will grow up overburdened by their parents' needs and consequently stunted in their own emotional and social development.

Equal to the effects of diminished parenting is the disruption of a relationship between a child and one parent. So often a divorce occurs in a parenting relationship as well as in the marriage. Making a clean break may meet the needs of parents who have separated, but it will not necessarily make life easier for children. The fact that mothers have day-to-day parental responsibilities for their children in 85–90 per cent of cases, and that within two years of separation less than half the non-custodial parents have regular access to their children (and a third have no contact with them at all) makes clear how vulnerable is the place of fathers after divorce. Moreover, the break from one parent may also mean the break from one set of grand-parents and one set of uncles, aunts and other relatives. Whereas bereave-ment is likely to bring together the wider family to support children, divorce may cut them off from family members who are seen as belonging to the 'other side'.

There is some consensus among the experts that when separated parents are able to work together, not to restore the marriage, but to ensure that their children enjoy a continuing relationship with each of them, the benefits for the children can be enormous, sometimes even greater than for children who come from unbroken homes. Protecting children from being drawn into the issues between the adults requires great maturity, but it pays handsome dividends in the long term. It is not the events of separation and divorce which are the crucial factors determining the effects upon children; it is the way these events are managed.

To summarize, the current state of knowledge suggests there are three main factors which mitigate the effects on children when their parents decide to part company: their continuing relationship with both parents free from the burden of divided loyalties, the quality of day-to-day care from the parent who remains in charge and the quality of what is created to take the place of the marriage.

As with bereavement, the changes which are hardest to manage are those which are unexplained and come without warning. One of the hardest burdens for children whose parents divorce is not knowing what is going on. The less they are told, the less they feel like asking and the more they rely on conjecture and fantasy. Information is a valuable resource which protects children from the extremes of helplessness when their world is being reorganized. Once a decision to part has been made, they will want and need to know. And if they are given a say in how to manage the arrangements which follow the break, they will feel both closer to the adults and more in control of their own destiny. This does not mean that children have to be burdened with knowledge and decisions which are relevant only to their parents, something which can occur when a parent is looking to the children for support and loyalty. Children only need to know about the things which affect them.

However, for parents to break the news of divorce constructively to their children requires a balance and reasonableness which may temporarily have deserted them. The unexpected and unexplained departure of a spouse can be as traumatic a shock for an adult as for the children. Adults too may have no opportunity to get used to the idea, to think about the implications and to begin to make alternative arrangements. Instead they may be overwhelmed by feelings of helplessness and outrage, and want to declare open war.

The sense of betrayal, which we discussed in the last chapter, will be keen. However necessary it may be to communicate, it is unreal to suppose that this will be easy when feelings are running high. Fear, anger and mistrust, combined with a general feeling of wanting to exclude one's partner, are powerful advocates for acting precipitately and unilaterally. The private satisfactions of 'showing him' or 'paying her back' may be too great to give up, but they can make a bad situation worse. Early discussion can hardly be expected to be easy in these circumstances and it is unlikely that partners will be able to make each other feel better about the prospects at that stage (although the fact that an intention is being shared may provide some reassurance about how matters will be handled in the future).

Both partners may be able to talk to others about what is likely to happen between them, and so to create the beginnings of a network of support outside the marriage. Friends and relatives can be alerted to the family's needs. Legal and practical advice can be helpful in managing the break rather than picking up the pieces of an acrimonious split. Some preventive action is possible. And there are many couples who have negotiated a new basis for their marriage simply by having come to the precipice of separation and talking about it.

But how are people helped to 'get into their own skins' sufficiently to decide whether they want to stay married or to part. It is to the question of seeking help that we now turn.

9. *Help*

TAKING THE DECISION

It is not unusual for married people to become so seriously concerned about the state of their relationship that they wonder about its future. Frequent quarrelling, neglect, sexual difficulties or problems in communicating can lead to the conclusion that something is fundamentally wrong. Attempts to discuss the situation together may fail. Reassurance from friends or family may not be forthcoming when informal attempts are made to sound them out. The hope that things will improve with time may fade as problems persist. What can be done that falls short of taking steps to end the marriage?

Marital problems are not always easy to define. Couples experience pressures and tensions in their relationship which originate from many different sources. A bad day at the office can lead to short-temperedness at home. The death of a family member, or a close friend, can result in one partner becoming self-preoccupied, depressed and unavailable to the other. The demands of young children can increase tetchiness and irritability in a partnership. All these pressures test the capacity of marriage to weather the stresses of everyday life and to deal with adversity. But they are not necessarily sufficient demonstration that it is the marriage which needs help. The short-tempered businessman may need to tackle the problem at work. The bereaved partner may need help in his or her own right if the course of grieving shows no signs of coming to an end. The hard-pressed parent may need practical help and support from outside the marriage. However, it may also be that through an improved marriage a couple will be better able to manage these pressures between them.

The decision about where to go for help is nearly always taken on the basis of how the problem is experienced and understood. Take, for example, a man who has difficulty obtaining and sustaining an erection during intercourse. He may respond in a number of different ways. He may believe there is something medically wrong with him and visit his doctor. He may discover as a result of tests that he has a diabetic condition which could account for the problem, or that the drugs he is taking for hypertension are having a dampening effect upon his ability to become sexually aroused. Either way, he has discovered a cause which fits his belief that something is medically wrong.

But it could very well be that no medical reason can be found. A different set of questions may then need to be asked. Is he expecting the same level of sexual activity at forty-five as he experienced at twenty-five? Is he looking for sexual reassurance that life is not passing him by? Is sexual performance being relied upon to bolster up a potency which is increasingly being threatened in other areas of life? If he does not entertain these questions he may choose to explain the problem in a manner which deflects attention away from himself. He may blame his partner for not taking sufficient interest in sex and suggest that she needs help. She may go along with this (either because she agrees or because she is willing to protect him by owning the problem) or she may become angry and even less responsive, and so aggravate the sexual problem. Most likely, there will be an interactive component of the problem to which one or other partner draws attention.

When a situation like this arises, couples need to ask themselves two kinds of questions. Firstly, they need to know what kind of problem they are facing. Is it an illness? Is it to do with a particular stage of life? Is it normal or should they be worried? Secondly, and closely related, they need to know where to locate the cause of the problem. Is it to do with us, or with something going on outside? If it's us, is it me or is it you? Because the relationship is so important to both of them, and self-esteem is so closely bound up with security in this area, these questions are infused with urgency. Finding the 'right' answer may become less important than finding any answer which offers reassurance.

But running alongside the need to find an answer to these questions is an equally strong wish not to know. People do not want to disturb their lives unless they really have to do so. Agencies offering counselling and therapeutic services are familiar with a drop-out rate (which can be as high as 50 per cent or more) between the time a couple telephones for an appointment and the offered date. Sometimes a complicated and offputting admission procedure is to blame. More often, the fall-out rate is related to mixed feelings about asking for help. It is not uncommon for one or both partners to have second thoughts.

The hope that someone may be able to change an unsatisfactory marriage is counterbalanced by a fear that the cost of change will be too high. Most of us prefer the devil we know to the unknown spectres of our imagination. Our innate conservatism, from which we derive some security, cautions against action which involves risks, unless, of course, we believe it is only our partner who needs to change and that the risk-taking will therefore be one-sided. If we think we are likely to become the object of attention, the person under pressure to change, we will tend to resist. And we resist for good reason. Change in one area of life has a knock-on effect. It can unsettle the confidence we have in ourselves and the prejudices we hold about those around us. Moreover there can be hidden benefits attached to the situations we complain most strongly about; for example, a secondary gain of illness is the attention it secures.

It is often difficult to credit that symptoms of disease can have a positive function. In the field of medicine we have become accustomed to thinking that ailments require cures, and to believing that the source of both ailment and cure lies outside ourselves.[1] We tend to become irritated and frustrated if we go down with a bout of 'flu' when we are overworking, as if the body has let us down when there is so much to be done. Yet the susceptibility of the body to illness can be seen as an asset, allowing us to know when life has got out of balance. The illness or symptom requires us to slow down in order that our balance may be regained and a sense of perspective restored. Frequently we just keep going and only discover how run down we have become when we stop for a holiday. Then we are prone to catch some infection and complain about having missed out on a proper holiday.

Physical symptoms are just as capable of drawing our attention to relationship difficulties. Some couples place undue value on having a conflict-free marriage and pride themselves on having similar views and outlooks on life. They may become anxious if they get into an argument with each other, believing that differences between them will spoil the value of what they have together. They may even fear that expressed differences will place their relationship in jeopardy. These beliefs may be underwritten by an interpretation of history which lays the blame for past relationship failures at the door of individual differences. The logic of the unconscious then dictates: 'If we were properly suited to each other he or she would understand how I am feeling and what I mean without my having to put it into words.' The same reasoning devalues what partners do for each other as a result of a request: 'Sex is no good if I have to ask for it.'

Not infrequently such couples do experience difficulties in their sexual relationship. They may seek help saying that everything between them is fine except for sex and offer that part of their relationship for treatment as if it were a foreign body quite disconnected from the rest of their lives. As we described in Chapter 5, sexual behaviour is a powerful means of expressing feelings in a relationship. Anger is as capable as love of dictating what does or does not happen. Sex also depends upon a degree of comfort with the physical and emotional differences between men and women. What is avoided in the day-to-day happenings of a relationship may surface unwelcomed in sex. But a sexual problem can be relied upon to signal that there are important but avoided issues in the relationship which require attention.

The link between physical and emotional disease is well established, although imperfectly understood. It is probable that many marital problems are first taken to doctors, although neither the doctors nor their patients may be aware of this. A survey of patients attending a doctor's surgery[2] estimated that 30 per cent had marital problems, one half of which were very severe. In many of these cases it is likely that an improvement in the marriage would have reduced or eliminated the physical symptoms for which help was being sought. The problem is that there is likely to be reluctance from both doctor and patient to reframe the nature of the disease. A physical symptom can be evidence of a patient's wish to see problems in medical rather than relationship terms, and the primary task of the doctor is to ensure that possible organic explanations are properly explored. The indirect nature of the presentation can indicate the degree of ambivalence about acknowledging that there is something amiss in a relationship which is so vital to personal security.

There are five common fears associated with seeking professional help. The first is whether the counsellor or therapist is competent at his or her job. As in all professions, including the medical and para-medical ones, there are varying levels of competence. The British Association of Counselling and the United Kingdom Council for Psychotherapy hold lists of registered practitioners, but there is still a choice to be made. Obviously, positive recommendation of a therapist and institution from others who have found help is one of the best signposts as to where to go. However, after an initial consultation, it is important to use one's own judgement as to whether this therapist is a person with whom one is prepared to invest money, time and emotional energy. Any consultation should be a two-way process, both therapists and couples weighing up whether they can work together.

Assuming the competence of therapist or counsellor, the second fear, a very normal one, is that if any outsider, however good at his job, is brought in, one will lose control. It may feel difficult to get this as yet unknown person to understand the situation properly. Will he be more sympathetic to one partner than the other? Will he have undue influence? Will he declare the marriage to have failed and suggest separation? Or will he insist that there must be reconciliation?

Associated with this anxiety is a fear of what might be revealed about oneself or one's partner, and a feeling that some things are better unsaid or unknown. Asking for help increases the level of uncertainty about what the future holds. For this reason many people delay seeking help until anxiety about what is happening to them outweighs the fear of losing control. Help may then be conceived of in terms of trying to put the clock back. Vernon Williams, who had been used to dictating the terms in his marriage and had been unable to hear the warning signals from his wife, asked for help only after she had left him and his efforts to recover her had failed. The help he wanted was for someone to do what he had been unable to do: to bring her back. He wanted to reinforce his control in the marriage rather than look at his own panic about losing the marriage and the security it had afforded him. The fear of losing control, which is commonly experienced when people are thinking of asking for help, can become quite specific (as in this case) where control has been an issue at the heart of the marital problem.

A third fear, closely associated with the second, is that the process will be damaging to the partner. The prospect of publicly exposing some of the things that have been privately bubbling inside, of doing some straight talking, can be formidable. Will he or she be terribly hurt by what I have to say? Will I be hurt? Perhaps it's better not to know: 'What the eye doesn't see the heart won't grieve over.' Will we simply antagonize each other further? Suppose we come to blows – literally or figuratively? The fear that things will end up worse than they were to start with can be a powerful deterrent against seeking help until the situation is really serious.

A fourth fear is concerned with trust. When a marriage is going wrong, partners feel particularly vulnerable to each other and to those who may offer help or advice from outside. Because the unwritten covenants we described in Chapter 4 have often been betrayed by one or other partner (either in relation to a third person or by changing in a way which does not allow the relationship to continue on its previous basis) trust can be at a very low level. Mistrust may be transferred to outsiders. Maybe an outsider will ally himself with one partner and manipulate the situation to his benefit. The more threatened we feel the more we demand absolute allegiance from those who offer to help: they are either for us or against us. The world can seem very persecuting and there is a temptation to fall back on the unconscious protective device of splitting described in earlier chapters. Doubts about our own trustworthiness are projected into others so that we can then question whether they can be trusted. We see in them the ruthlessness or exploitiveness we fail to see in ourselves: or we may deride their impotence and ineffectiveness in order to protect ourselves from the knowledge of our own feelings of helplessness.

In making a commitment to counselling or therapy a couple is likely to stir up feelings which are linked with the degree of confidence they have in others to be of help. Past experience may incline them towards keeping a sceptical distance. Or they may plunge into a precipitate commitment in the belief that some magical formula will become available. But the question of whether or not others can be trusted with what is most precious will never be far from the surface.

A fifth factor which can inhibit asking for help is connected with the way we see ourselves. When we are feeling ill and decide to consult a doctor we have to undergo a change of identity. From being healthy members of the community we have come to terms with ourselves as patients. Usually the transition is not difficult to make because no blame is attached to being ill. No stigma results from seeing a doctor, and we expect that some brief treatment will quickly restore us to our former selves. The same does not apply when relationships run into difficulties. Feelings of personal failure, injustice, hurt and bitterness accompany the change. It takes an effort to concentrate on the most mundane activities, and it is often with a sense of shame, humiliation and guilt that the step is taken to seek help. Such a change of state is often more difficult for men than for women. By and large, it is women who take their courage in their hands and go and talk to someone about the problems in their marriage.

The fear of receiving help means that the decision to call in outside assistance is seldom taken without misgiving and is always accompanied by ambivalent feelings. Given the nature of what goes on between couples, ambivalent feelings are quite likely to be polarized. Her determination to obtain help may lead him to dig his heels in. His reluctance to talk about the problem may drive her into seeking help unilaterally. As a result she may 'protect' him from knowing about his own concern about the marriage while he may 'protect' her from knowing of her own misgivings about calling in help. If the polarization is extreme it may sabotage any attempts to make use of what help is available. The best prognosis follows from couples having been able to agree upon seeking help together and upon where they go to obtain it. This, in turn, involves them in thinking about the nature of their problem and the kind of expectations they have of the help they wish to receive. Sometimes perceptions and expectations will coincide, often they will be very different. Discussing these differences will normally be part of the work done in the early stages of any professional help a couple may receive. But because people are usually rather hazy about what to expect when they turn to others for help it is worth exploring the realistic options as well as the personal hopes.

EXPECTATIONS

From what we have said so far we hope it will be clear that going for help with one's marriage is not like going to the doctor with an illness. There are no clearly defined categories of marital problem with readily identifiable causes which can be treated and cured. There are no solutions which can be applied from outside and have only to be 'swallowed' to provide a remedy. By its very nature marriage is affected by the individual personalities of the partners and the environment in which they live out their lives together. Tension in marriage derives from a complicated interplay between what lies inside and what lies outside. It is only when this interplay generates unbearable tensions that the marriage is threatened. Help is then required to recover a balance in the partnership which can be maintained in the face of these pressures. Or help may be used to discover that no such balance is possible and the partners may need to go their separate ways with the least possible damage to themselves and others. Either way, the analogy of priest may be more apposite than that of a doctor to describe what the therapist is trying to do (in so far as priests concern themselves with the pursuit of meaning and spiritual integrity).

When help is sought from a specialist who is seen to be in authority, it is not surprising that feelings about other authority relationships are evoked. In particular, there are likely to be very strong feelings about where the responsibility lies for what happens in a therapeutic encounter. Someone who is approached for help may be given the tag of 'expert'. The belief may be that he or she needs only to know the full story and an answer will be forthcoming. The responsibility for the problem can then be transferred, and a passive expectancy greets the hapless counsellor, who feels a rabbit must now be drawn out of the hat.

In contrast, there are people who feel so uncertain about whether they have the right to expect anything that they fail to press any claims at all. Instead they may try to read what is expected of them and to conform to what they think the counsellor expects them to say and do. Either way, something important is communicated about the way people manage their relationships. The degree of discomfort experienced when asking for help, although influenced by the context in which a request is made, may say something about what can and cannot be asked for in a marriage. A panic call for help which bypasses waiting lists and normal procedures can communicate the degree of anxiety there is about the situation. A unilateral approach to an agency for help may say something about how a couple communicates (or fails to) in their relationship. In short, the message is as frequently in how people behave as in what they say.

Outside help is turned to for a variety of reasons, not all of them concerned with looking for a better way of managing problems. Probation officers (who provided marriage guidance services twenty and thirty years ago) used to tell of women who would come to see them complaining bitterly about violent or spendthrift husbands in the hope that an officer of the court would write a reprimanding letter to their husbands. People frequently see solicitors – even file petitions for divorce – in the hope of shocking their partners into line. Those who are convinced the problem lies with their partner may attend counselling sessions in order that he or she shall be given the treatment thought to be needed. Even people who are desperately anxious to improve their marriage can have an unconscious wish for the counsellor or therapist to fail; it is not easy to accept that others may succeed where one has failed without feeling even more of a failure as a result.

Perhaps we have said enough to show that what people expect of the help they seek is fashioned not only by the services which are available but also by conscious and unconscious fantasies triggered on the one hand by the nature of the problem being experienced and on the other by the juxtaposition of need and authority inherent in the helping relationship. Now we shall say a little about what the helpers think are realistic expectations of the helping process.

Among the range of organizations and individuals who offer therapeutic services to couples there are three broad divisions of emphasis. Firstly, there are those who address the symptom or complaint that couples bring to their attention primarily by devising and monitoring self-help programmes.[3] If John Bull is complaining that his wife Catherine is not paying him sufficient attention, specific behavioural techniques can be learned which may remedy the situation. For example, John and Catherine may be encouraged to list their dissatisfactions and bargain with each other to improve the situation between them. Behavioural therapies come closest to the medical model in their approach to helping marriages, and they are used frequently for specific sexual problems, such as premature ejaculation and orgasmic difficulties. As we described in Chapter 5, carefully planned programmes aim to lower anxiety levels before embarking on graded exercises which may overcome the identified problem in a relationship.[4]

There are also approaches which focus on the relationship between a couple, examining not only what needs and emotions each partner expresses for the other but also deciphering the purposes each serves for the other by the part they play in the relationship. The marriage is seen primarily as a self-contained system and the emphasis is on changing the balance in the relationship to secure a better equilibrium.[5] John and Catherine may be encouraged to come closer together in order that they may experience whether or not they like or want a different level of intimacy. What they say they want as individuals will be placed beside what they can manage in their partnership. Help consists of encouraging them to test how much more they can manage together.

Then there is our own psychoanalytic approach which recognizes the power of unconscious motives and early blueprints. The emphasis is on the two individuals *in the partnership* and how, because of the unconscious factors in the original choice, they fit together. Particular attention is, therefore, paid to the interactive system – shared fears and shared defences – which a couple have set up together, and to personal histories and relationships within their own families of origin in order that connections between present problems and past experiences can be explored and understood. John and Catherine Bull may each be seen individually, as well as together, to give them an opportunity to speak about their dissatisfactions and explore them in relation to experiences of intimacy in other relationships.[6] Perhaps John and Catherine both come from large families where there was not enough attention to go round. They may have entered marriage in the search for a parent, hoping that their partner would make up for what had been missing from their childhood, only to discover that this was not possible. Help focuses upon coming to terms with what is unchangeable in the past, and distinguishing that from what may be changed in the present.

We have separated these three approaches to try to illustrate what those who help marriages will be looking for and at in their endeavours. In practice, the boundaries between the approaches will not be clear cut. A combination of perspectives is likely to be used, especially in relation to the last two, but each hybrid will draw heavily on one of the three routes.

One disappointment frequently expressed by couples who seek help for their marriage is that they are not given advice. There is often an expectation that once the problem has been described some clear and practical advice will be forthcoming. Sometimes advice is given, but its usefulness is often much less than imagined. In the first place, when you are not part of the marriage in which a problem is being experienced, the solutions which may seem appropriate to you as an outsider are not necessarily those which will be of help to those on the inside. Counsellors and therapists have always to be on their guard against reading too much of themselves into the situations presented to them. Secondly, it is extremely difficult to know whether the advice will be heard in the way and the spirit it was intended. Through long experience helpers have come to learn how advice can be abused and misunderstood to the detriment of the helping process. In the troubled climate of a marital crisis it is not difficult for the partners to hear a suggestion that they spend a little more time apart as a judgement that the marriage has no future. Thirdly, advice-giving perpetuates an illusion that there are external solutions which can be applied to the problems which couples are facing. In fact, effective solutions which are to have a chance of surviving and being built upon have to come from inside. Couples must *own responsibility* for their problems and the means they adopt to manage them.

We have referred to counselling and psychotherapy as distinct activities. The difference between them may not be clear. Indeed, they have much in common. Both use the helping relationship as a vehicle for change. Both require that keen attention is paid to spoken and unspoken communications. And both seek to keep the responsibility for change in the hands of the couple. However, the objectives of marital psychotherapy are more ambitious than those of counselling. Attempts are made to effect fundamental change, not only in the marriage but in the individuals themselves, often using the experience of the relationships between couples and therapists as the primary means for this purpose, as well as working with what happens outside the therapeutic context. Because of this, marital psychotherapy usually lasts longer than counselling and involves more frequent meetings.

Yet the difference between the two activities is one of degree rather than kind. Both operate on the assumption that what is started in the interviewing room will be continued by the couple in the interval between appointments.

Many agencies now produce written information about the kind of help they offer. Although this is most likely to describe the parameters of the help available – frequency and length of sessions, the intake or consultation process, financial arrangements – it is well worth obtaining a description of what is available and discussing this fully at the first appointment. However, the experience of help can really only be known about in retrospect. The personal nature of the service means that it is not possible to know in advance how the experience will turn out.

WHERE TO GO

At the end of this book we have listed some organizations which can be approached for help and further information about where help is available. It is not a comprehensive list and will not take account of all the organizations which provide local services, or the many individuals who offer counselling or therapy for marriages and families on a private basis.

A broad distinction can be made between the different kinds of help which are available. There are education programmes directed towards those who are contemplating marriage. There is help for those who are married or living together. And there are services for those who are in the process of ending their partnership. These components are not watertight. Those receiving help for their marriage may end up deciding to separate. Those wanting help to separate may end up deciding to stay together. The same organizations may offer all three kinds of help or they may specialize in one.

Programmes of education for marriage and family life are not widely available. Where they are available they are likely to be directed either towards children as part of a school curriculum or to couples who intend to marry. Programmes which are part of a school curriculum will be of a more general nature than those directed towards engaged couples. Although these programmes may include information about contraception and discussion about sexual behaviour (and this is often a sensitive area about which parents and teachers are likely to have strong views), they are likely to encourage children to think about the whole range of relationships in which they are

174

involved at that time. Any anticipation of life after marriage is likely to be rooted in family experiences they have already had, although programmes may include expectations of and fantasies about marriage. In contrast, programmes designed for couples who are planning to marry will be more focused, encouraging partners to assess how well they know each other and to be explicit about what they expect. Some organizations also offer marriage enrichment courses.

Counselling and psychotherapy for couples are available from both specialist and non-specialists agencies. We have described many of the assumptions which lie behind the work they do. Most organizations are quite explicit about the fact that their objective is not necessarily to save marriages, but to help couples eventually come to a considered decision about the future of their relationship, either by implementing change or discussing what cannot be changed.

The most recent services for couples are those designed to assist people with the process of separation. In western countries the rapid rise in divorce is a phenomenon of the last twenty years. The 1969 Divorce Reform Act in England and Wales extended the range of individual choice about whether or not to stay in marriage and reflected a change in culture by substituting 'irretrievable breakdown' in place of proof of a 'matrimonial offence' as the sole legal criterion for divorce. Currently there are proposals for reforming the divorce law once again, to remove the remaining vestiges of 'fault' and to focus attention away from proving the ground to addressing the consequences of divorce. While it takes more than legislation to diminish the notion of there being a guilty party when marriage breaks down, attitudes are changing and there is recognition of the fact that, collectively, we often make the process of parting more difficult and damaging than it need be.

Two kinds of service are geared specifically to the needs of those who are separating. There is divorce counselling and there is mediation. Marriage guidance agencies have long counselled those in the throes of leaving marriage, but because these agencies are often associated in the public mind with mending marriage they have not been used as frequently as they might. In consequence, a small number of specialist services have been set up to address the specific needs of individuals who are in the process of separation and divorce. While they may offer much needed practical advice, they will also try to help people manage the emotional impact of the break and come to terms with the consequences of the change they have embarked upon.

Quite separation from divorce counselling is mediation. In this country mediation was pioneered in Bristol in the late 1970s with the intention of providing an alternative to litigation for settling the important practical issues which attend divorce. While mediation services do not usurp the role of solicitors, nor bypass legal procedures, they do allow couples, and sometimes families, to meet together on neutral territory to discuss specific practical decisions which need to be taken and about which there may be dissent. Essentially, mediation allows the couple to negotiate their own solutions. Child custody and access issues are often key components of this process. Agreement in these areas arrived at through mediation can then be presented to the courts for ratification. This is clearly preferable to fighting over differences through prolonged and costly legal battles.

By offering a brief and tightly focused service, mediation can be very helpful to couples who are in danger of coming to blows over practical decisions which have to be taken when a marriage breaks down. There are services available in most parts of Britain, but they are less well developed than those in the USA, Australia and New Zealand. Sometimes mediation is offered quite independently of the courts before litigation has started; sometimes it is available in the precincts of the court after an application has been filed.

Very often it happens that people are not sure exactly what kind of help they want and find it difficult to be precise about the nature of their problems. Then, the array of different kinds of service can add to the confusion. While we have drawn divisions between different kinds of service in order to describe the provision available in most western countries, it is true to say that most of those who offer services to couples recognize how difficult it can be for people to be clear about what they want, and will see it as part of their job to help clarify the issues involved. It is not necessary, therefore, to be too concerned about knocking on the wrong door. What is important to note is that in addition to the priest, the doctor and the lawyer, there are others who can offer specialist help to marriages in trouble.

Last, but not least, there are a growing number of books, magazine articles and television and radio programmes which aim to provide information, advice and a sounding-board for people who want to understand more about what is happening in their marriage without necessarily taking the step of calling in outside help. We hope that this book will fall into this category of help and shed light on what goes on within and between ordinary people who choose to live together in the rewarding but frequently problematic commitment of marriage.

Epilogue

In this book we have written about some of the problematic issues that arise in most marriages at one time or another. We have described how for some people these issues can escalate into Marital Problems. In the last two chapters we have written about parting company and seeking outside help, two courses of action open to those whose marriages are stressed beyond their own resources.

However, most marriages do not founder on the rocks of adversity. Despite the divorce rate having risen so sharply over the last twenty years, at least three out of five marriages will survive until the death of one partner in old age and many will have provided until then the greatest source of strength, comfort and pleasure for both partners. Research has demonstrated that through the different seasons of married life a strong, mutually supporting and satisfying marital relationship is one of the most significant factors in the health and well-being of the partners and any children they may have. In this sense the 'mutual society, help and comfort' that marriage can provide is critically important to the physical and emotional health of the community.

At this time in history, when the balance between personal choice and collective responsibility tips in favour of the individual, diversity is tolerated; partners are relatively free to work out together how they will support and sustain each other and what is right for them as individuals and as a pair. True, the burden of responsibility upon the individual is then greater, and the support which derives from social convention is less, but the effect can be liberating. Marriage can publicly sustain the different degrees of intimacy that people find most comfortable. No longer does a couple's decision to maintain separate homes have to be construed as evidence that they are not getting along together. There is no longer a requirement for gender roles to be rigidly defined. There are opportunities for men and women to realize their potential inside and outside the home, and plenty of room for these opportunities to be taken up. The complexity of life in the closing years of this century demands a flexible and adaptive response from people.

Although we have written about the inherently problematic nature of intimate relationships, particularly in the context of a changing social climate which exerts its own pressures on individuals and families, 'problematic' does not have to carry a negative connotation. Life without challenge, without the struggle to understand, solve and overcome, would be boring indeed. Much of this struggle to develop goes on quite unselfconsciously. Many people are able to use their innate good sense, flexibility and confidence in themselves to negotiate the problem of married living without undue fuss and drama. They are able both to care and cherish, and to allow themselves to be cared for and cherished. Problems then become less problematic. Current events may often reverberate painfully on old wounds and some people will feel the reverberations more acutely than others, but the struggle – even strife – which is set in train does not have to become a Problem. It can be the start and means of growth.

The commitment of marriage evokes ambivalent reactions. As a social institution it has been blamed for oppressing women, causing physical and emotional ill-health, precipitating delinquent behaviour and inhibiting the development of wider community relationships. But it has also been credited with giving individuals a sense of place and purpose in life, with fostering health through emotional security, and perpetuating a sense of morality and civilization. At a personal level this ambivalence is replicated. Most of us go through periods when we wish to break out of what can feel like the shackles of marriage, but we are also longingly and lovingly drawn back to this important relationship. Perhaps it is only to be expected that we should, collectively and individually, be ambivalent towards an institution which at both public and private levels is concerned with balancing the need to conserve with the pressure to change.

Marriage matters because it flushes out the personal meaning of committed intimacy and because it provides a socially buttressed forum in which change and development can occur. Despite that constant damnable clutter on the kitchen table, and sometimes because of it, love can thrive as much on the ordinary and the mundane as in the grand passion. The best marriages do not have to sustain that 'extraordinary hallucination' of the perfect match, but can support individual differences within the framework of a working partnership. And such marriages, as Ogden Nash attests, are not a rare species:

> I know that marriage is a legal and religious alliance entered into by a man who can't sleep with the window shut and a woman who can't sleep with the window open.

Moreover, just as I am unsure of the difference between flora and fauna and flotsam and jetsam,

I am quite sure that marriage is the alliance of two people one of whom never remembers birthdays and the other never forgetsam,

And he refuses to believe there is a leak in the water pipe or the gas pipe and she is convinced she is about to asphyxiate or drown,

And she says, Quick get up and get my hairbrushes off the windowsill, it's raining in, and he replies, Oh they're all right, it's only raining straight down.

That is why marriage is so much more interesting than divorce,

Because it's the only known example of the happy meeting of the immovable object and the irresistible force.

Notes

1. THE MARRIAGE MAZE

1. For a historical review of marriage in Britain see Gillis, J. R., *For Better For Worse: British Marriages 1600 to the Present*, New York and Oxford, Oxford University Press, 1985.
2. *Marriage Matters* (A Consultative Document by the Working Party on Marriage Guidance), London, HMSO, 1979.
3. The conflict between public and private interests during divorce is discussed by Clulow, C., and Vincent, C., *In the Child's Best Interests? Divorce Court Welfare and the Search for a Settlement*, London, Tavistock, 1987.
4. See, for example, Young, M., and Willmott, P., *The Symmetrical Family*, Routledge & Kegan Paul, 1973, and Rapaport, R. and R., *Dual Career Families*, Harmondsworth, Penguin Books, 1971.
5. Bernard, J., *The Future of Marriage*, Harmondsworth, Penguin Books, 1976. (First published 1972 by Wales Publishing, New York.)
6. Gorer, G., *Sex and Marriage in England Today*, London, Nelson, 1971.
7. Bott, E., *Family and Social Network*, 2nd ed., London, Tavistock, 1971.
8. Both phrase and theme were developed by A. C. R. Skynner in *One Flesh, Separate Persons; Principles of Marital and Family Psychotherapy*, London, Constable, 1976.

    The theme is further explored by Robert Morley in *Intimate Strangers*, London, Family Welfare Association, 1984, and A. Mann in *The Human Paradox*, Rugby, National Marriage Guidance Council, 1974.
9. This point was first made by one of our colleagues, Alison Lyons, and used by her in an unpublished paper.

2. BLUEPRINTS

1. Bowlby, J., *Attachment and Loss*, 3 vols, London, Hogarth Press and Institute of Psycho-Analysis: vol. 1, *Attachment*, 1969; vol. 2, *Separation, Anxiety and Anger*, 1975; vol. 3, *Loss: Sadness and Depression*, 1980.
2. James and Joyce Robertson have produced five films on the responses of young children to separation; they are available from the Tavistock Institute of Human Relations, the Robertson Centre and the New York University Film Library.
3. Bowlby, J., *Attachment and Loss*, op. cit., vol. 1, *Attachment*.
4. For graphic illustrations of children's development through play see Fraiberg, S.

H., *The Magic Years*, New York, Scribner, 1959, and Winnicott, D. W., *Playing and Reality*, Harmondsworth, Penguin Books, 1974.

5. See, for example, Freud, S., 'Three Essays on the Theory of Sexuality' (1905) in the Standard Edition of the *Complete Psychological Works of Sigmund Freud*, vol. VII, London, Hogarth Press, 1953, pp. 125–245.

6. The role of fathers in families is relatively neglected in psychological writing. See McKee, L., and O'Brien, M., eds, *The Father Figure*, London, New York, Tavistock, 1982.

7. Robin Skynner and John Cleese describe this journey in their book *Families and How to Survive Them*, London, Methuen, 1983.

3. CHOICES

1. Emery, F. E., and Trist, E. C., *Towards a Social Ecology*, London, Plenum Press, 1972.

2. Haley, J., ed., 'Conversations with Milton H. Erickson', in *Changing Couples*, vol. 2, New York, Triangle Press, 1985.

3. See Stevenson, A., *Archetype: A Natural History of the Self*, London, Routledge & Kegan Paul, 1982. Lily Pincus also made this point, describing marriage as the 'direct heir' to childhood relations, in Pincus, L., ed., *Marriage: Studies in Emotional Conflict and Growth*, London, Institute of Marital Studies, 1960.

4. See Segal, H., *Introduction to the Work of Melanie Klein*, London, Heinemann Medical Books, 1964.

4. COMMITMENT

1. Jung, C. G., 'Marriage as a Psychological Relationship', in *Collected Works*, vol. 17, London, Routledge & Kegan Paul, 1931.

2. Searles, H. F., 'Oedipal Love in the Countertransference' in *Collected Papers on Schizophrenia and Related Subjects*, London, Hogarth Press, 1959.

5. INTERCOURSE

1. Quoted by Freud in 'Group Psychology and the Analysis of the Ego', Standard Edition, vol. XVIII, London, Hogarth Press and the Institute of Psycho-Analysis, 1955.

2. Byng-Hall, J., 'Resolving Distance Conflicts', in Gurman, A. S., ed., *Casebook of Marital Therapy*, New York and London, Guilford Press, 1985.

3. Jung, C. G., 'Psychological Types', in *Collected Works*, vol. 6, London, Routledge & Kegan Paul, 1920.

4. Masters, W. H., and Johnson, V. E., describe their treatment formula in *Human Sexual Inadequacy*, London, Churchill, 1970.

5. Friedman, L. J., *Virgin Wives, A Study of Unconsummated Marriages*, London, Tavistock, 1968.

6. SHOCKS TO THE SYSTEM: PREDICTABLE EVENTS

1. See Holmes, T. H., and Rahe, R. H., 'The social readjustment rating scale', *Psychosomatic Research*, 11 (1967), 213–18.
2. Peter Marris in his book *Loss and Change* (Routledge & Kegan Paul, 1974) draws attention to the ambivalence essential to any major transition because of the struggle to maintain a continuity of meaning between the new and the old.
3. Brown, G. W., and Harris, T., *Social Origins of Depression*, London, Tavistock, 1978.
4. See, for example, Gavron, Hannah, *The Captive Wife*, Harmondsworth, Penguin Books, 1968.
5. Jackson, B., *Fatherhood*, London, Allen & Unwin, 1984.
6. For some examples of this the reader is referred to Christopher Clulow's book, *To Have and to Hold: Marriage, the First Baby and Preparing Couples for Parenthood*, Aberdeen University Press, 1982.
7. For a discussion on the relationship between home and work see Janet Mattinson's book, *Work, Love and Marriage: The Impact of Unemployment*, London, Duckworth, 1988.

7. SHOCKS TO THE SYSTEM: BETRAYAL

1. Williams, H. A., *True Resurrection*, London, Fount Paperbacks, 1972.
2. Parkes, C. M., *Bereavement: Studies of Grief in Adult Life*, 2nd ed., Harmondsworth, Penguin Books, 1986.
3. Marris, P., *Loss and Change*, London, Routledge & Kegan Paul, 1974.
4. See Pincus, L., *Death in the Family*, London, Faber, 1976.
5. Ashton, J. R., 'The psychosocial outcome of induced abortion', *British Journal of Obstetrics and Gynaecology* (1980), 87.
6. Bowlby, J., *Attachment and Loss*, vol. 1, *Attachment*, London, Hogarth Press and Institute of Psycho-Analysis, 1969.
7. Blomberg, B. D., *et al.*, 'The psychological sequelae of abortion performed for a genetic indication', *American Journal of Obstetrics and Gynaecology* (1975), p. 122.
8. Peppers, L. G., and Knapp, R. J., *Motherhood and Mourning: Perinatal Death*, New York, Praeger, 1980.
9. *Social Trends*, London, HMSO, 1994.
10. Caplan, G., *An Approach to Community Mental Health*, London, Tavistock, 1961.
11. Klein, M., *Love, Hate and Reparation*, London, Hogarth Press, 1937.
12. Beale, N., and Nethercote, S., 'Job loss and family morbidity: a study of a factory closure', *Journal of the Royal College of General Practitioners* (Nov. 1985), 35.
13. Platt, S. D., 'Unemployment and suicidal behaviour', *Social Science and Medicine* (1984), 19.
14. Veitch, A., *Guardian*, 5 July 1986. He reported delay in the publication of a politically sensitive document.

15. Haskey, J., 'Grounds for divorce in England and Wales. A social and demographic analysis', *Journal of Biosocial Sciences* (1986), 18.
16. Mattinson, J., *Work, Love and Marriage: The Impact of Unemployment*, London, Duckworth, 1988.
17. Haskey, J., op. cit.
18. Hillman, J., 'Betrayal', in *Loose Ends: Primary Papers in Archetypal Psychology*, Zürich, Spring Publications, 1975.
19. See Fader, J. R., 'The Transitional Person: Understanding Infidelity', *Marriage Guidance*, 20, 2 (1982), 75–80.
20. *Social Trends*, London, HMSO, 1988.

8. PARTING COMPANY

1. See Maclean, M., and Eekelaar, J., *Children and Divorce: Economic Factors*, Oxford Centre for Socio-Legal Studies, 1983 and Maclean, M., *Surviving Divorce*, London, Macmillan, 1991. The Institute of Fiscal Studies has recently published a report arguing for a change in the law to allow all financial gains and liability (including property and pension rights) to be shared equally after divorce: Freeman, J., *et al.*, *Property and Marriage: An Integrated Approach*, London, Institute of Fiscal Studies, 1988.
2. The emotional reactions to separation and divorce, and how they impinge upon and are affected by the legal system, are portrayed in *Parting Company*, a training video produced by the Tavistock Marital Studies Institute in 1988 as a stimulus for disucssion between parents and professionals.
3. For a description of the social dislocation which follows marriage breakdown see Hart, N., *When Marriage Ends: A Study in Status Passage*, London, Tavistock, 1976.
4. Robert Weiss's book *Marital Separation*, Basic Books, New York, 1975, gives a good account of the emotional reactions to marital breakdown.
5. Ambrose, P., Harper, T., and Pemberton, R., *Surviving Divorce: Men Beyond Marriage*, Brighton, Wheatsheaf Books, 1983.
6. Martin Richards discusses the impact of divorce on children in Burgoyne, J., Ormrod, R., and Richards, M., *Divorce Matters*, Harmondsworth, Penguin Books, 1987.
7. Wallerstein, J. S. and Kelly, J. B. *Surviving the Breakup: How Children and Parents Cope with Divorce*, London, Grant McIntyre, 1980.

9. HELP

1. A classic contribution to discussions about the psychological function of illness was made by Michael Balint in his book *The Doctor, His Patient and the Illness*, London, Pitman Medical, 1964. More recently, David Smail has addressed the subject in *Illusion and Reality: The Meaning of Anxiety*, London, J. M. Dent, 1984.
2. Renst, J., Golombok, S., and Pickard, C., 'Marital Problems in General Practice', *Sexual and Marital Therapy*, 2, 2 (1987).

3. Some self-help exercises are listed in *Staying Together* by Beech, R., Chichester, Wiley & Sons, 1985.
4. W. H. Masters and V. E. Johnson pioneered this approach and describe their work in *Human Sexual Response*, London, Churchill, 1966. K. Hawton writes more recently in *Sex Therapy: A Practical Guide*, Oxford University Press, 1985.
5. A systems perspective on helping marriage is described in John Byng-Hall's paper, 'Resolving Distance Conflicts', in Gurman, A. S., ed. *Casebook of Marital Therapy*, New York and London, Guilford Press, 1985.
6. The Tavistock Marital Studies Institute describe this approach in their series of publications on helping marriages. See for example, Clulow, C., *Marital Therapy: An Inside View*, Aberdeen University Press, 1985 and Ruszczynski, S. (ed.), *Psychotherapy with Couples*, London, Karnac, 1993.

For a review of all three approaches to helping marriages see Dryden, W., ed. *Marital Therapy in Britain*, vols. I and II, London, Harper & Row, 1985 and Hooper, D. and Dryden, W. (eds.), *Couple Therapy: A Handbook*, Buckingham, Open University Press, 1991.

Further Reading

Askham, J., *Identity and Stability in Marriage*, Cambridge, Cambridge University Press, 1984

Bannister, K., and Pincus L., *Shared Phantasy in Marital Problems*, London, Tavistock Marital Studies Institute, 1965

Beech, R., *Staying Together*, Chichester, Wiley & Sons, 1985

Bernard, J., *The Future of Marriage*, Harmondsworth, Penguin Books, 1976

Bowlby, J., *A Secure Base*, London, Routledge, 1988

Brannen J., and Collard, J., *Marriages in Trouble: The Process of Seeking Help*, London, Tavistock, 1982

Burgoyne, J., *Breaking Even: Divorce, Your Children and You*, Harmondsworth, Penguin Books, 1984

Burgoyne, J., and Clark, D., *Making A Go of It: A Study of Stepfamilies in Sheffield*, London, Routledge & Kegan Paul, 1984

Burgoyne, J., Ormrod, R., and Richards, M., *Divorce Matters*, Harmondsworth, Penguin Books, 1987

Clark, D. and Haldane, D., *Wedlocked*, Cambridge, Polity Press, 1990

Clark, D., *Marriage, Domestic Life and Social Change*, London, Routledge, 1991

Clulow, C., *To Have and to Hold: Marriage, the First Baby and Preparing Couples for Parenthood*, Aberdeen, Aberdeen University Press, 1982

Clulow, C. (ed.), *Rethinking Marriage: Public and Private Perspectives*, London, Karnac, 1993

Clulow, C., *Marital Therapy: An Inside View*, Aberdeen, Aberdeen University Press, 1985

De'Ath, E. and Slater D., *Parenting Threads: Caring for Children when Couples Part*, London, National Stepfamily Association, 1992

Dicks, H., *Marital Tensions*, London, Tavistock, 1967

Dryden, W., *Marital Therapy in Britain*, vols. I and II, London, Harper & Row, 1985

Fraiberg, S. H., *The Magic Years*, New York, Scribner, 1959

Gillis, J. R., *For Better For Worse: British Marriages 1600 to the Present*, New York and Oxford, Oxford University Press, 1985

Gurman, A. S., ed., *Casebook of Marital Therapy*, New York and London, Guildford Press, 1985

Hart, N., *When Marriage Ends: A Study in Status Passage*, London, Tavistock, 1976

Hawton, K., *Sex Therapy: A Practical Guide*, Oxford, Oxford Univeristy Press, 1985

Hooper, D. and Dryden, W., *Couple Therapy: A Handbook*, Buckingham, Open University Press, 1991

James, A., and Wilson K., *Couples, Conflict and Change: Social Work with Marital Relationships*, London, Tavistock, 1986

Mansfield, P., and Collard, J., *The Beginning of the Rest Of Your Life? A Portrait of Newly Wed Marriage*, London, Macmillan, 1988

Marris, P., *Loss and Change*, Routledge & Kegan Paul, 1974

Mattinson, J., *Marriage and Mental Handicap*, London, Duckworth, 1970

Mattinson, J., *Work, Love and Marriage: The Impact of Unemployment*, London, Duckworth, 1988

Mattinson, J., and Sinclair, I. *Mate and Stalemate: Working with Marital Problems in a Social Services Department*, Oxford, Blackwells, 1979

Morley, R., *Intimate Strangers*, London, Family Welfare Association, 1984

Pape-Cowan, C. and Cowan, P., *When Partners Become Parents*, USA, Basic Books, 1992

Parkes, C. M., *Bereavement: Studies of Grief in Adult Life*, 2nd ed., Harmondsworth, Penguin Books, 1986

Pincus, L., *Death in the Family*, London, Faber, 1976

Pincus, L., and Dare, C., *Secrets in the Family*, London, Faber, 1978

Reibstein, J. and Richards, M., *Sexual Arrangements: Marriage and Affairs*, London, Heinemann, 1992

Ruszczynski, S., *Psychotherapy with Couples*, London, Karnac, 1993

Skynner, A. C. R., *One Flesh, Separate Persons: Principles of Marital and Family Psychotherapy*, London, Constable, 1976

Skynner, A. C. R., and Cleese, J. *Families and How to Survive Them*, London, Methuen, 1983

Wallerstein, J. S., and Kelly, J. B., *Surviving the Breakup: How Children and Parents Cope with Divorce*, London, Grant McIntyre, 1980

Weiss, R., *Marital Separation*, New York, Harper & Row, 1975

Winnicott, D. W., *Playing and Reality*, Harmondsworth, Penguin Books, 1974

VISUAL MATERIAL

Tavistock Marital Studies Institute/Skippon Video Associates, *Parting Company: The Impact of Separation and Divorce*, 1988

Tavistock Marital Studies Institute/Skippon Video Associates, *Unemployment and Marriage*, 1988

Useful Addresses

Asian Family Counselling Service
74 The Avenue
London W13 8LB

Association for Marriage Enrichment
23 Kensington Square
London W8 5HN

Association of Sexual and Marital Therapists
PO Box 62
Sheffield S10 3TS

British Association for Counselling
1 Regent Place
Rugby
Warwicks. CV21 2PJ

Catholic Marriage Advisory Council
1 Blythe Mews
Blythe Road
London W14 0NW

Cruse-Bereavement Care
Cruse House
126 Sheen Road
Richmond
Surrey TW9 1UR

Exploring Parenthood
Latimer Education Centre
194 Freston Road
London W10 6TT

Families Need Fathers
c/o 42 Drury Lane
London WC2B 5RN

Family Mediators Association
The Old House
Rectory Gardens
Henbury
Bristol BS10 7AQ

Family Policy Studies Centre
231 Baker Street
London NW1 6XE

Family Welfare Association
501–505 Kingsland Road
London E8 4AU

Gingerbread
35 Wellington Street
London WC2E 7BN

Institute of Family Therapy
43 New Cavendish Street
London W1 7RG

Jewish Marriage Council
23 Ravenshurst Avenue
London NW4 4EE

London Marriage Council
76a New Cavendish Street
London W1M 7LB

Marriage Counselling Scotland
26 Frederick Street
Edinburgh EH1 2JR

Mothers Apart from Their Children (MATCH)
c/o BM Problems
London WC1N 3XX

National Association of Citizens Advice Bureaux
115–123 Pentonville Road
London N1 9LZ

National Council for One Parent Families
255 Kentish Town Road
London NW5 2LX

National Family Mediation
9 Tavistock Place
London WC1H 9SN

One Plus One, Marriage and Partnership Research
Second Floor, 12 New Burlington Street
London W1X 1FF

Relate – Marriage Guidance
Herbert Grey College
Little Church Street
Rugby CV21 3AP

Samaritans
17 Uxbridge Road
Slough SL1 1SN

Scottish Institute of Human Relations
56 Albany Street
Edinburgh EH1 3QR

Solicitors' Family Law Association
Secretary, P. H. Grose Hodge
PO Box 302
Orpington
Kent BR6 8QX

Stepfamily (National Step-Family Association)
162 Tenison Road
Cambridge CB1 2DP

The Tavistock Clinic
Tavistock Centre
120 Belsize Lane
London NW3 5BA

Marriage Inside Out

Tavistock Marital Studies Institute
Tavistock Centre
120 Belsize Lane
London NW3 5BA

United Kingdom Council for Psychotherapy
Regents' College
Regents Park
London NW1 4NS

Westminster Pastoral Foundation
23 Kensington Square
London W8 5HN

Index